A Leadership Guide to Navigating the Unknown in Education

Recognizing that education systems have been temporarily paralyzed in the past and likely will in the future—whether it's because of a natural disaster or a pandemic—this important volume offers critical insights about how schools can effectively carry forward the mission of educating all children even in the face of system turbulence and disruption.

Featuring Narratives from expert leaders in urban, rural, and suburban school systems, this book explores important questions about the "new normal" such as the ways in which students can and should learn, how educators can teach and lead effectively, and how schools can carry out important functions beyond their instructional mission. Chapters present inspiring stories of leaders and teachers who have rallied, rebuilt, and problem-solved in the face of the pandemic and amid adversity, ultimately providing a roadmap for how it's possible to rebuild and adjust while preserving the fundamental core of education. Full of takeaways and first-hand insights into how systems and their schools faced turbulence, disruption, and adaptation, this book is a must-read for today's educators committed to making a positive impact on the students they have the duty to serve.

Sally J. Zepeda is a Professor of Educational Administration and Policy at the University of Georgia, USA.

Philip D. Lanoue is an Educational Consultant and former 2015 American Association of School Administrators (AASA) National Superintendent of the Year.

Also Available from Sally J. Zepeda and Philip D. Lanoue

Developing the Organizational Culture of the Central Office: Collaboration, Connectivity, and Coherence
Sally J. Zepeda, Mary Lynne Derrington, and Philip D. Lanoue

Professional Development: What Works (3rd Edition)
Sally J. Zepeda

The Leader's Guide to Working with Underperforming Teachers: Overcoming Marginal Teaching and Getting Results
Sally J. Zepeda

Job-embedded Professional Development: Support, Collaboration, and Learning in Schools
Sally J. Zepeda

Informal Classroom Observations on the Go: Feedback, Discussion, and Reflection (3rd Edition)
Sally J. Zepeda

The Principal as Instructional Leader: A Handbook for Supervisors (3rd Edition)
Sally J. Zepeda

Instructional Supervision: Applying Tools and Concepts (4th Edition)
Sally J. Zepeda

Supervision Across the Content Areas
Sally J. Zepeda and R. Stewart Mayers

Instructional Leadership for School Improvement
Sally J. Zepeda

A Leadership Guide to Navigating the Unknown in Education

New Narratives Amid COVID-19

Sally J. Zepeda and
Philip D. Lanoue

NEW YORK AND LONDON

First published 2021
by Routledge
52 Vanderbilt Avenue, New York, NY 10017

and by Routledge
2 Park Square, Milton Park, Abingdon, Oxon OX14 4RN

Routledge is an imprint of the Taylor & Francis Group, an informa business

© 2021 Taylor & Francis

The right of Sally J. Zepeda and Philip D. Lanoue to be identified as authors of this
work has been asserted by them in accordance with sections 77 and 78 of the Copyright,
Designs and Patents Act 1988.

All rights reserved. No part of this book may be reprinted or reproduced or utilised
in any form or by any electronic, mechanical, or other means, now known or
hereafter invented, including photocopying and recording, or in any informations
torage or retrieval system, without permission in writing from the publishers.

Trademark notice: Product or corporate names may be trademarks or registered trademarks,
and are used only for identification and explanation without intent to infringe.

Library of Congress Cataloging-in-Publication Data
A catalog record for this title has been requested

ISBN: 978-0-367-56284-7 (hbk)
ISBN: 978-0-367-56375-2 (pbk)
ISBN: 978-1-003-09744-0 (ebk)

Typeset in Optima
by Newgen Publishing UK

Contents

About the Authors ... ix
Preface ... xi
Acknowledgments ... xx

Chapter 1: Framing Unprecedented Disruptions ... 1
    Introduction ... 1
    A New Journey Begins ... 2
        Narrative: *Together, We Can Do This* ... 5
    The Context of Disruption ... 9
        Narrative: *When You Least Expect It…* ... 11
    The Influence of Social Media ... 14
    New Trajectories ... 16
    Leading for Tomorrow ... 21
    References ... 22

Chapter 2: Teachers and Leaders Care First for Their Students ... 24
    Introduction ... 24
    The Absence of Traditional School Structures ... 25
        Narrative: *You Are Not Alone* ... 26
    Parents Assume Different Roles ... 34
        Narrative: *Supporting Parents and Caregivers*
            During Uncertain and Disruptive Times ... 35
    Meeting the Unique Needs of Children ... 38

Contents

Narrative: *Learning to Work with Tools
from a New Toolbox: Student Supports During
COVID-19* 42
Leading for Tomorrow 45
References 46

Chapter 3: Short-term Response, Long-term Implications 50
Introduction 50
Responding to Students' Basic Needs 51
Narrative: *Agility and Adaptability: Two Keys to
Future Success* 53
Creating New Systems 56
Narrative: *The COVID-19 Impact on School Design* 60
The New Normal 64
Narrative: *Disruption Accelerates Transformation
and Strengthens Community* 67
Leading for Tomorrow 72
References 73

Chapter 4: Teaching as We Knew It 75
Introduction 75
Traditional Conventions 76
Narrative: *72 Hours: The Year with No
Good-Byes* 78
Teaching, Learning, and the Schoolhouse 82
Narrative: *Adapting Instruction in the "New Normal"* 84
Human Connections 88
Narrative: *Relationships Can Thrive During a Crisis* 90
Leading for Tomorrow 96
References 97

Chapter 5: Supporting Social and Emotional Needs 99
Introduction 99
Student Growth and Social Development 100
Narrative: *Supporting Student Social Emotional
Wellness During a Time of Isolation* 103
Social Dynamics of Schools 106
Narrative: *Lessons Learned While Navigating
the Unknown* 111

Contents

New Thinking Moving Forward	114
Narrative: *We Really Did Own It*	117
Leading for Tomorrow	122
References	123

Chapter 6: The Roles of Schools and Their Communities ... 127

Introduction	127
Community Relationships	128
Narrative: *Leveraging Local Leadership During a Global Crisis*	130
Schools and Healthy Children	135
Narrative: *Communities Respond in Uncharted Territory*	137
Student Well-being in a Virtual Environment	142
Narrative: *Leading for Wellness When All is Not Well: Lessons from COVID-19*	143
Leading for Tomorrow	147
References	147

Chapter 7: Leading Through the Unknown ... 149

Introduction	149
Pivoting Decisions Rapidly	150
Narrative: *System Priorities Keep You Focused During Crisis Leadership*	154
Leveraging Resources	157
Narrative: *COVID-19—Thank Goodness for Strong Finance Officers!*	159
Shifting Traditional Systems	163
Narrative: *Back to the Future?*	164
Leading for Tomorrow	169
References	170

Chapter 8: Education in America *Will* Change ... 172

Introduction	172
The Journey Continues	173
Teachers, Parents, and Leaders Care	174
From System Rigidity to System Flexibility	176
Moving Forward is a Choice	177

Contents

Unspoken Responsibilities	178
Power of Community	179
A New Normal	181
Gateway to a Brighter Future	182
Narrative: *Education During the Pandemic — Lessons and Opportunities*	183
The Next Chapter in the Journey	187
Index	191

About the Authors

Sally J. Zepeda, Ph.D., is a Professor in Educational Administration and Policy at the University of Georgia where she teaches courses and conducts research related to instructional supervision, professional development, and teacher evaluation. Before entering higher education, Dr. Zepeda served as a high school English and speech teacher, director of special programs, assistant principal, and principal.

Dr. Zepeda has worked with many school systems in the United States and overseas, especially in the Middle East, to support teacher and leader development. She has designed teacher and leader evaluation systems, instructional coaching programs, model system-wide strategic plans as well as degree and academic programs.

Philip D. Lanoue, Ph.D., has a demonstrated record in leading school transformation at the building and district levels. Dr. Lanoue is the 2015 American Association of School Administrators (AASA) National Superintendent of the Year, as well as the 2015 Georgia Superintendent of the Year. Before serving at the superintendent level across two systems, Dr. Lanoue was a high school principal in Vermont, leading four schools toward excellence, and he was named Principal of the Year by the Vermont National Association of School Principals.

Dr. Lanoue continues to serve as a voice advocating for public education and children. He has served on the White House Policy Advisory for the New Generation High School Summit and the ConnectED Future

About the Authors

Ready White House Summit. Dr. Lanoue co-authored *The Emerging Work of Today's Superintendent: Leading Schools and Communities to Educate All Children* with Dr. Sally J. Zepeda (Rowman & Littlefield and jointly published by the American Association of School Administrators).

Preface

 ## Approaches Running Throughout This Book

We began the journey of writing this book in late March 2020 as systems and their schools closed their doors and moved to virtual spaces. Writing about the unknown and the decisions made by leaders was a challenge as shifts evolved frequently and quickly. We spent our time interacting with system and school leaders across several states, watching and reading about what was occurring in schools and their communities, and observing the social disruptions across the country. From these experiences, we gained insights about how systems and their schools faced turbulence, disruption, and adaptation.

The approaches running throughout this book are situated in practice. Each of the chapters will:

- examine a critical area of schooling by focusing on their function pre-COVID-19—insight will then be offered regarding how these areas had to change to fit the present realities in which schools and systems found themselves;
- present Narratives that address the changes in practice and thinking from system leaders, school leaders, and/or leaders from national organizations—these Narratives capture lessons learned that can guide systems in educating children in the face of turbulence, disruption, and adaptation, whether it's due to pandemic or another disruptive force;
- articulate and amplify the new thinking needed to lead systems, their schools, and communities for new tomorrows.

Preface

Through examining and amplifying change and the complexities of decision-making, the chapters open opportunities to guide systems, schools, and their communities in the introspection and rethinking that support short- and long-term planning for whatever the "new normal" brings to bare.

Objectives of the Book

The primary objective of this book was to examine as much as we know about the disruptions that schools, systems, and their communities experienced by the COVID-19 pandemic. The COVID-19 pandemic is far from over, and other disruptions will evolve as systems work through what is best for their students and communities. Although the writing of the book stopped in mid-November, we gained many insights about the efforts of school districts and schools to ensure students had the opportunity to continue with learning. Social media, newspaper articles, and blogs remind us of the challenges leaders faced, and the many victories along with their failures along the way.

The second objective was to illustrate decision-making and the complexities that system and school leaders, parents, and communities experienced as they journeyed through spring 2020 to fall 2020. There was no playbook to guide leaders, systems, and their communities in making decisions. There was no professional experience for school personnel to draw from as they faced system turbulence. The magnitude of decisions that had to be made could not be neatly teased from decision-making theories learned in educational leadership preparation programs, professional learning seminars, or well-meaning self-help books.

Yet, school systems responded within days to continue educating children.

The third objective was to understand how leaders balanced new information on COVID-19, emerging public opinion, an intense political environment, and student and staff safety with effective instructional practices. Critical decisions regarding whether to open face-to-face in fall 2020 needed to be made around the health and emotional wellness of the students and teachers, the steep learning curves for teachers to change instructional practices, and the ever-present press.

Preface

The fourth objective was to underscore the dynamics of school and organizational leadership through insights by educational leaders from across the country. These perspectives provided insights about the challenges of leading through the COVID-19 pandemic amplified by local, state, and federal politics, geographical locations, school size, levels of COVID-19 cases, school funding deficits, and equity gaps.

Book Features

In *A Leadership Guide to Navigating the Unknown in Education: New Narratives Amid COVID-19*, each chapter includes approximately three **Narratives** written by a slate of thought leaders in the K-12 space as well as national organizations. By reviewing the Narratives, the reader will see that the professionals are representative of urban, rural, and suburban school systems across the United States.

The Narratives provide concrete examples of the concepts, ideas, and strategies discussed in the chapters. The contributors offer their insights from the practices that they enacted during COVID-19, the lessons they learned while leading during a pandemic, and how the focus on what they learned will influence the future of their systems. Through these Narratives we see what systems and leaders did to "make education work," and how systems project their thinking to actions to better educational opportunities for students.

At the conclusion of each chapter, key takeaways are offered and attention is drawn to the major ideas offered in the section entitled, **Leading for Tomorrow**. These takeaways as well as the questions embedded in each chapter serve as starting points to further the conversations about what is possible as systems and schools move forward.

What's Inside the Chapters?

The content of *A Leadership Guide to Navigating the Unknown in Education: New Narratives Amid COVID-19* spans eight chapters. The chapter annotations serve to acquaint the reader with the contents of each.

xiii

Preface

Chapter 1: Framing Unprecedented Disruptions

In "Framing Unprecedented Disruptions," the emerging influences on public education from COVID-19 are outlined with a chronology to help understand and engage educators in navigating the emerging influences and the context influencing decision-making with the understanding of new educational trajectories. Key messages from parents, students, teachers, and national thought leaders help leaders to understand the full impact of schools and the decisions made during this pandemic.

- Introduction
- A New Journey Begins
  - Narrative: *Together, We Can Do This*
- The Context of Disruption
  - Narrative: *When You Least Expect It…*
- The Influence of Social Media
- New Trajectories
- Leading for Tomorrow
- References

Chapter 2: Teachers and Leaders Care First for Their Students

In "Teachers and Leaders Care First for Their Students," the impact of the COVID-19 pandemic on the traditional structure of schools, the new role of parents, and the impact on the unique social, emotional, and learning needs of students are explored. Schools needed to pivot quickly in seeking new ways to meet the growing social and emotional impact on students when schools closed, the challenges as parents became teachers, and equity and access arose in the evolving virtual learning environment.

- Introduction
- The Absence of Traditional School Structures
  - Narrative: *You Are Not Alone*

xiv

Preface

- Parents Assume Different Roles

  - Narrative: *Supporting Parents and Caregivers During Uncertain and Disruptive Times*

- Meeting the Unique Needs of Children

  - Narrative: *Learning to Work with Tools from a New Toolbox: Student Supports During COVID-19*

- Leading for Tomorrow
- References

Chapter 3: Short-term Response, Long-term Implications

In "Short-term Response, Long-term Implications," quick responses were required to respond to the needs of students while creating a level of continuity amid program modifications and the implementation of new delivery models. School leaders and teachers evaluated current systems with a lens of safety as they developed and implemented a new teaching and learning environment that was fast becoming the new normal.

- Introduction
- Responding to Students' Basic Needs
  - Narrative: *Agility and Adaptability: Two Keys to Future Success*
- Creating New Systems
  - Narrative: *The COVID-19 Impact on School Design*
- The New Normal
  - Narrative: *Disruption Accelerates Transformation and Strengthens Community*
- Leading for Tomorrow
- References

xv

Preface

Chapter 4: Teaching as We Knew It

In "Teaching as We Knew It," the sudden shift to a fully virtual environment disrupted almost every traditional convention known to schools from instructional delivery models and class schedules to how teachers and students remained connected. Rethinking the framework in schools defined by contracts, influenced by high-stakes testing, and founded on face-to-face interactions required new and different conversations leading to new definitions and approaches.

- Introduction
- Traditional Conventions
  - Narrative: *72 Hours: The Year with No Good-Byes*
- Teaching, Learning, and the Schoolhouse
  - Narrative: *Adapting Instruction in the "New Normal"*
- Human Connections
  - Narrative: *Relationships Can Thrive During a Crisis*
- Leading for Tomorrow
- References

Chapter 5: Supporting Social and Emotional Needs

In "Supporting Social and Emotional Needs," the concerns about the well-being of students and their social development became a primary focus equally as important as academic loss and gains as schools made decisions to reopen, remain in a virtual environment, or a hybrid combination of both. As schools reevaluated the events of the spring and the needs moving forward, supporting the gaps in students' social learning and growth while supporting the well-being of teachers required a new level of intensity and intentionality.

- Introduction
- Student Growth and Social Development
  - Narrative: *Supporting Student Social Emotional Wellness During a Time of Isolation*

- Social Dynamics of Schools
  - Narrative: *Lessons Learned While Navigating the Unknown*
- New Thinking Moving Forward
  - Narrative: *We Really Did Own It*
- Leading for Tomorrow
- References

Chapter 6: The Roles of Schools and Their Communities

In "The Roles of Schools and Their Communities," the COVID-19 challenges permeated well beyond the schoolhouse boundaries and into communities causing disruption to multiple systems requiring a need to forge new working relationships and collective decision-making. Schools, community agencies, and government entities needed to work in tandem. They needed to come together as decisions were made and communicated to ensure targeted interventions met the mental wellness needs of students.

- Introduction
- Community Relationships
  - Narrative: *Leveraging Local Leadership During a Global Crisis*
- Schools and Healthy Children
  - Narrative: *Communities Respond in Uncharted Territory*
- Student Well-being in a Virtual Environment
  - Narrative: *Leading for Wellness When All is Not Well: Lessons from COVID-19*
- Leading for Tomorrow
- References

Chapter 7: Leading Through the Unknown

In "Leading Through the Unknown," leaders were positioned to make decisions about complex problems resulting from a changing COVID-19

Preface

pandemic. Decisions were often hotly intertwined in politics spanning local and national levels. Finding a way through the divided thinking about school safety and emerging academic models, lack of resources, and the potential of permanently changing education as known historically created "no win" situations for school leaders across the country.

- Introduction
- Pivoting Decisions Rapidly
  - Narrative: *System Priorities Keep You Focused During Crisis Leadership*
- Leveraging Resources
  - Narrative: *COVID-19—Thank Goodness for Strong Finance Officers!*
- Shifting Traditional Systems
  - Narrative: *Back to the Future?*
- Leading for Tomorrow
- References

Chapter 8: Education in America Will Change

In "Education in America *Will* Change," the totality of what schools have endured and the multiple responses to a changing pandemic environment are summarized using the Narratives from among the strongest educational leaders across the country. These responses to COVID-19 do not define a return to business as usual but rather point to an ongoing journey that will test the ability for systems to change and adapt.

- Introduction
- The Journey Continues
- Teachers, Parents, and Leaders Care
- From System Rigidity to System Flexibility
- Moving Forward is a Choice
- Unspoken Responsibilities

- Power of Community
- A New Normal
- Gateway to a Brighter Future
  - Narrative: *Education During the Pandemic—Lessons and Opportunities*
- The Next Chapter in the Journey

Acknowledgments

There are many people who supported the writing of this book, and we are indebted to their good will and graciousness.

First, we thank Vickie G. Lanoue whose artwork depicting the COVID-19 pandemic became the book cover.

Several teachers, parents, and school-aged children shared their experiences about schooling in light of the COVID-19 pandemic. We needed their voices, and they delivered—without reservation.

We are indebted to the professionals who wrote Narratives, 21 in all, spanning Chapters 1 through 8. Their voices and calm resolve serve as examples of courageous leadership. From these Narratives, we gain keen insight about the future based on the lessons they shared with us. These voices made this book possible:

- Dr. Jill A. Baker, Superintendent: Long Beach Unified School District (Long Beach, CA)
- Dr. Mary Elizabeth Davis, Superintendent: Henry County Schools (McDonough, GA)
- Dr. Daniel A. Domenech, Executive Director: AASA (Alexandria, VA)
- Dr. Mark Elgart, President/CEO: COGNIA (Alpharetta, GA)
- Dr. Susan Enfield, Superintendent: Highline Public Schools (Burien, WA)
- Dr. Douglas Huntley, Senior Associate: CSArch (Albany, NY)
- Dr. Stephen Joel, Superintendent: Lincoln Public Schools (Lincoln, NE)
- Dr. Joey N. Jones, Principal: Robert Frost Middle School—Montgomery County Public Schools (Rockville, MD)

Acknowledgments

- Dr. Katherine Kelbaugh, Executive Director: The Museum School of Avondale Estates (Decatur, GA)
- Dr. Nardos King, Assistant Superintendent, Region 3: Fairfax County Public Schools (Falls Church, VA)
- Dr. Michael Lubelfeld, Superintendent: Northshore School District 112 (Highland Park, IL)
- Mr. Jeff McCoy, Associate Superintendent for Academics: Greenville County Schools (Greenville, SC)
- Mr. Rich Merlo, Superintendent: Corcoran Joint Unified School District (Corcoran, CA)
- Dr. Dawn Meyers, Social Emotional Learning Specialist: Foothills Education Charter High School (Athens, GA)
- Mr. Robert A. Morales, Retired Chief Financial Officer (Acworth, GA)
- Dr. Armand Pires, Superintendent: Medway Public Schools (Medway, MA)
- Dr. Grant Rivera, Superintendent: Marietta City Schools (Marietta, GA)
- Dr. Donald E. Robertson, Jr., Chief Strategy and Innovation Officer: Virginia Beach City Public Schools (Virginia Beach, VA)
- Dr. Susan Stancil, Principal: Dove Creek Elementary School—Oconee County School District (Statham, GA)
- Dr. Brian Troop, Superintendent: Ephrata Area School District (Ephrata, PA)
- Dr. Calvin J. Watts, Superintendent: Kent School District (Kent, WA)

Working diligently behind the scenes were Sevda Yildirim and Salih Çevik, both Ph.D. candidates in the Department of Lifelong Education, Administration, and Policy at the University of Georgia. They stood ready to assist—and they did—in so many ways from start to finish. Thank you is not enough to express our gratitude.

Heather Jarrow, Publisher with the Routledge/Taylor and Francis Group, provided insights and counsel from inception to completion. We appreciated the organization and attention to detail provided by Rebecca Collazo, Senior Editorial Assistant, Education.

Thank you,

Sally J. Zepeda, Ph.D.
Philip D. Lanoue, Ph.D.

Framing Unprecedented Disruptions

In This Chapter...

Introduction	1
A New Journey Begins	2
Narrative: *Together, We Can Do This*	5
The Context of Disruption	9
Narrative: *When You Least Expect It...*	11
The Influence of Social Media	14
New Trajectories	16
Leading for Tomorrow	21
References	22

 ## Introduction

We are in the midst of an event that this country and world has never faced—a worldwide pandemic that has shuttered students from school as they knew it. Questions of in-school or not, virtual or not, safe or not are now amplified. These would appear to be questions that school leaders should readily and emphatically be prepared to answer. The disruptions and multiple decisions that had to be made and then remade as information became more available have almost paralyzed systems to carry forward their missions.

This chapter examines the multiple contexts to understand and engage in navigating the emerging influences in decision-making. Broadly examined are the disruptions and ruptures that dominated the context of COVID-19 in schools and their systems. Key messages from parents, students, and teachers are offered as a way to hear their voices.

A New Journey Begins

The year 2020 and the COVID-19 pandemic have tested the mettle of teachers, building and system leaders, parents, and students. The school year ended with countless losses in traditional school experiences for students and their communities. Students did not come to closure—they missed proms, graduation ceremonies, and saying good-bye to their teachers in person. The journey for schools and their systems was just beginning as COVID-19 continued to spread.

The complexities of COVID-19 were exacerbated by strong periods of unrest tipping conversations around issues that have caused turbulence, disruption, and subsequent needs for adaptation in local, state, and national policies and perspectives. These new disruptions sent strong messages for immediate and long-term changes. But changes to what, in an unknown world? The following highlights the journey of schools to "pivot" their efforts to serve students.

Spring 2020

In March 2020, school systems began closing their schools, and by May, just about every school across the United States had shut their doors. As a result, by the time school began for fall 2020, most students had missed approximately 25% of the 2019–2020 school year. Couros (2020) reminds us that "As a world, we are experiencing loneliness together" (para. 8) and Magee (2020) tells us succinctly:

> What we need to focus on now is how to meet the immediate needs of students. That means accepting we have a new mission, identifying the problems standing in the way of success, and rapidly trying out new solutions until we find the ones that help us achieve this mission.
>
> (para. 2)

However, there was no playbook to consult.

COVID-19 forced unprecedented decisions that immediately and fundamentally changed every school in this country. The longest standing tradition of going to the schoolhouse in the morning was severed indefinitely as a measure to thwart the spread of COVID-19. Quickly, school systems mobilized their resources in ways that were unprecedented and within days, teachers taught in ways that were foreign to them and their students. Teachers scrambled to convert face-to-face lessons and content to the online environment, and they used platforms to collaborate to develop strategies to connect with students and their parents. New ways of communicating evolved for teachers, students, and parents.

Principals coordinated with teachers to bring logic to their immediate school community of teachers, students, and parents. District leaders oversaw efforts seeking waivers for breakfast and lunch programs, creating systems to deliver counseling and health services, and examining technology infrastructures to reimagine instruction and the efforts of teachers. School cafeteria workers worked behind the scenes to make breakfast and lunches and stood in line as parents picked up food for their children, and in many systems, bus drivers followed their routes to drop off food, and buses were equipped to act as hotspots in their communities. In addition, communities pitched in by making hotspots accessible to students.

In March, Congress allocated $13.2 billion to K-12 schools as part of its stimulus package, the Coronavirus Aid, Relief, and Economic Security Act, known as the CARES Act. Grants went to states based on ESEA Title 1-A funds. The intent of this funding was to support school systems to cover unexpected costs such as "cleaning and sanitizing schools, purchasing educational technology including laptops and hotspot devices, training educators to use online learning tools, ensuring access to education for students with disabilities, and providing students emergency funding for food, housing, and other basic essentials" (Committee on Education & Labor, 2020, p. 1).

These first steps, albeit not perfect, maintained a level of confidence in the ability of districts to engage students who were not physically in their school buildings. The hope—that the changes made were temporary and short-term—were crushed as COVID-19 numbers climbed over the summer months necessitating rethinking how schools would open for fall 2020.

Framing Unprecedented Disruptions

Summer 2020

Fast-forward to summer 2020. There was no clear answer to when children would return fully in person. The preparation continued to be in flux as the summer moved into fall 2020. Teachers, parents, and other stakeholders could not wrap their minds around the rapid-fire decision-making that was occurring with superintendents, school boards, and community agencies.

Through the trail of this pandemic, it became clear at the onset that school systems and the structures of learning needed to change for the short term and for the long run, albeit unknown. Leaders and teachers needed to rely on their experiences with openness to move forward with the new thinking to adapt to future events that may also cause disruptions to educating children. The only constant we must hold onto and embrace are relationships. Wheatley prophetically predicted that relationships serve to stabilize systems that are facing new futures with unknown outcomes:

> It is possible to prepare for the future without knowing what it will be. The primary way to prepare for the unknown is to attend to the quality of our relationships, to how well we know and trust one another.
>
> (Wheatley, 2003, p. 190)

Systems were tested even more as plans for fall 2020 evolved.

Fall 2020

Fall 2020 was the gateway to the year, beginning the foray into what schools would evolve to become. The COVID-19 pandemic was unfolding as we wrote. So different from any event in our experience, the COVID-19 virus sees all alike. The impact across the globe was universal and not separated by nationalities, languages, cultures, or education levels. As a writing team, we followed numerous ruptures as communities experienced both surges and declines in virus outbreaks. These ruptures required multiple cycles of contingency planning where leaders engaged in predicting scenarios with incessant "stop, drop, and replan." Multiple scenarios had to be built because current information within the span of a day eclipsed plans that were barely 24 hours old. One superintendent shared, "Things are nuts, and superintendents have become daily punching bags for all the

Framing Unprecedented Disruptions

anger from learning, politics, athletics, and anything else someone wants to assign to us. I'm absolutely exhausted."

Many systems were resolute about students returning to school face-to-face. These valiant attempts for students to return were often upended by surges and spikes in the spread of this virus. Numerous schools that started quickly had to return to virtual models. Many parents remained vocal about their children returning to school regardless of the number of COVID-19 cases and whether they wore masks or not. Systems experienced further disruption when students exposed to the virus had to go into quarantine for up to two or more weeks. Fall 2020 was marked by many starts and stops to routines creating uncertainties for students and their parents who held the often-conflicting responsibility to supervise their child at home in a virtual setting while having to work. For district leaders, responding to the immediate disruption from COVID-19 and preparing for an unknown future may have been the most significant challenge in their careers.

Dr. Susan Enfield is the superintendent of Highline Public Schools (HPS) located in Burien, Washington. HPS serves 19,287 K-12 students supported by 1,125 classroom teachers and 2,704 staff. Currently in her ninth year serving as superintendent in Highline, Dr. Enfield is the 2020 recipient of the AASA Women in School Leadership Award and was named the 2018 National Superintendent of the Year by the National School Foundation Association.

In her Narrative, Dr. Enfield relied on her system's core values, while connecting to people and modeling strength, vulnerability, and honesty. Dr. Enfield's message is that as "leaders we have always had the responsibility of being purveyors of hope, but never has that been more needed, or challenging to do, than in 2020."

Susan Enfield, Ed.D.
Superintendent
Highline Public Schools
Burien, WA

Together, We Can Do This

During one of my first Zoom visits to a high school class, this phrase was hanging on the Bitmoji classroom wall:

Framing Unprecedented Disruptions

You have to get up every morning and say to yourself: "I can do this."

I can't think of a sentiment that better sums up the reality for those of us leading school systems through a global pandemic. As leaders, we have always had the responsibility of being purveyors of hope, but never has that been more needed, or challenging to do, than in 2020.

Those of us who choose to dedicate our lives to public education get up each day believing the impossible is possible. I never realized how true these words were until March 12, 2020—the last day that students in Highline Public Schools were physically in our buildings. In the months since then, leaders have had to navigate an ever-changing landscape of public health guidance and conflicting information and opinions on when and how to reopen schools. At times, it has most definitely felt that we were being asked to do the impossible. And yet, we keep getting up every morning to do the best we can.

Leading in this moment while preparing for a future filled with far more uncertainty than we have ever known, I have found myself relying on a few key strategies that, while not new, have become essential in the era of COVID-19.

Our Lifeline: Connect With and Through Our Shared Core Values

In 2012 when I first joined Highline, the leadership team was reading *The Pedagogy of Confidence* by Yvette Jackson. Dr. Jackson's research centers on the question, "what if we treated every child as gifted?" As a teacher, I had always committed to knowing my students by name and need and continued this focus into my career as an administrator. What I also believed in, but hadn't intentionally named, however, was the need to know students' strengths as well. In this moment the Highline Promise was born: knowing every student by name, strength, and need so they graduate prepared for the future they choose. In the years since then, this promise has become the DNA of our system and our collective why.

When we had to close schools, it was important to help staff, students, and families remain connected and confident that our school communities, while virtual, remained intact. Returning again and again to our promise was a constant reminder of what binds us together: our shared core values of equity, relationships, and support. We rallied to ensure that our students had devices, home Internet, food, and social-emotional and academic support. While so much was changing around us, our Highline Promise was a reminder of who we were and that we could get through this together. Connecting with core values is, and always will be, central to good leadership. In times of crisis, upheaval, and uncertainty, however, it becomes a lifeline.

Prioritize What Matters Most: People

One day last spring I was taking an exercise class and heard the instructor say, "what we are going for here is persistence not perfection." Exactly, I thought! I immediately shared it with my Highline community on social media and have since repeated it in many messages to staff.

We talk so much about systems. What we sometimes lose sight of is that systems are made up of people. In times of crisis, people need to know that their leaders have their well-being at the center of every decision.

Given all of the unknowns and very real health concerns associated with contracting COVID-19, Highline staff, families, and students were, and are, understandably fearful for their personal safety. Communicating all of the steps we were taking as a district to keep them safe—from closing schools, to enforcing mask wearing and physical distancing—was critically important. So, too, however, was promoting and modeling self-care.

One of my long-time leadership mantras in Highline has been health and family first. Always. I have worked hard to remind people of this and model for them how important it is to exercise, eat well, spend time with family, rest, and do things that bring you joy. Physical health is important, but so too is mental health and now—living in semi-isolation and abandoning familiar routines—our physical and mental health are inextricably linked. As leaders, telling people to take care of themselves only has meaning if we can show that we are doing it ourselves. Acknowledge how challenging some days are and remind people that this is a marathon, not a sprint. *Our students need us to care for ourselves, so we can care for them.*

Make Time to Consciously Recalibrate

Disequilibrium feels like a constant state of being for leaders today, and my cabinet has struggled to establish our new ways of working together. It was feeling overwhelming until one day when our Chief Talent Officer, Steve Grubb, provided us with an analogy that perfectly captured our current leadership challenge. Up until March, we as a leadership team in Highline were playing checkers. And we were really good at checkers—we might

Framing Unprecedented Disruptions

even say that we had mastered checkers. But the game has changed. And it has no name and no rulebook. Yet, we are still playing checkers by the same old rules that we know. That won't get us through this, nor will it help us create a better system moving forward.

As a leadership team, we had to spend time mourning the loss of our old habits, routines and strategies, and work to create new ones. It was painful but also liberating once we realized that we had the power to recalibrate, as a team, and that in some ways, we were better than before. We have become more honest and precise now in naming what we need from one another and are clearer on our collective goals, and how we will reach them.

Model Strength, Vulnerability, and Honesty

This is one of the highest impact strategies we can use. Leadership is all about modeling—we never ask anything of our teams that we won't do ourselves, and we always walk our talk. In recent months I have grown weary, even impatient, with those who keep pushing the narrative of "We got this." Leading through a global pandemic is not something any of us studied in graduate school and so we were completely unprepared for this new reality. As such, there are days when I have felt completely overwhelmed, sad, angry. As leaders we must inspire hope and confidence, but we must also model humanity. Letting our staff know that we struggle, just like they do, demonstrates empathy and honesty. People appreciate seeing their leaders as human, and humanity is more important than ever before.

Focus on the Future

As all-consuming as our present may be, we must also help people see that one day this will be in our rearview mirror and we will have the opportunity—and responsibility—to apply what we have learned to improve public education for our children.

Many are talking now about the transformation that will occur within public education as a result of what COVID-19 has forced us to do. While I am hopeful that we will not return to the outdated, inequitable practices that too often defined us pre-COVID-19, I also know that the muscle memory of a bureaucracy, like public education, is strong. The pull to return to what we have always known and done will be great.

Transformation is by no means guaranteed—it will be hard won and require us to fight for equity, for our children, in ways we have not before. That, however, should energize us all and compel us to consciously and collaboratively design the schools our children deserve rather than simply wait for change to happen. The future is ours to design now. In that, I find great hope and reason to get up each morning.

Together, we can do this.

In the trenches, all leaders struggled with pushing through the pandemic, but Dr. Enfield brought hope and optimism to "demonstrate empathy and honesty" with the resolve and courage to redefine education moving forward. Dr. Enfield aptly concluded that "Together" communities must be opportunistic in rethinking practices that bring equity to the forefront in the mission of supporting every student in new ways.

Dr. Enfield's message is important because teachers, parents, and other stakeholders could not wrap their minds around the rapid-fire and ever-changing decision making that was occurring with superintendents, school boards, and community agencies. The disruptions brought by COVID-19 were complicated by other social dilemmas and uprisings.

The Context of Disruption

Schools and their systems are not immune to larger social issues (e.g., Black Lives Matter and police actions) or climate changes and natural disasters (Hurricane Sally, the loss of the ice shelf in Greenland, and rampant fires in California). Political entanglements divided the country with a highly contested presidential race between Republican incumbent Donald J. Trump and Vice-President Michael R. Pence and Democratic presidential hopeful Joe Biden and running mate, U.S. Senator Kamala Harris. The United States was on high-alert when President Trump was hospitalized for COVID-19 following the first presidential debate.

Highlighting a long history of social injustice and adding to the disruption of the pandemic were past and recent racial unrest that unfolded as cities experienced protests over police actions and the recent deaths of

Breonna Taylor in Louisville, Kentucky (March, 2020) and George Floyd in Minneapolis, Minnesota (May, 2020), and the shooting of Jacob Blake, who was left paralyzed in Kenosha, Wisconsin (August, 2020). The American public was polarized even further when President Trump at the presidential debate in October 2020 refused to denounce white supremacists, telling the public to "stand back and standby." These tragedies coupled with others have plummeted our country into periods of anguish and rage that continued as courts weighed their verdicts on police actions.

While public education has always been influenced after a presidential election, the changes foreseen with President Biden and a new educational cabinet may well create a breath of fresh air as education has endured without national direction or support in educating all students in this country. Under President Biden, federal funding more than likely will not be siphoned off to private and religious schools, and public schools will see a greater national role in adequately supporting and recognizing the importance of their work. Among many systems dismantled under the Trump administration, a movement to restore national influences on college affordability, sexual assault policies, and a return to protective rights of teachers and students are examples that have substantive impact on the future of our education system.

A new lexicon emerged to capture the work around the pandemic. The *Oxford Dictionary* added COVID-19 in the online format; the dub, Covidiot—a non-practicing person using safety and health protocols—as well as infodemic surfaced. Words such as "pivot" and "grace" and phrases including "a new normal" and "scenario planning" were uttered as teachers, leaders, parents, and students tried to make sense of their new and foreign conception of schools.

Leaders had to decipher a great deal of scientific data and findings from medical reports from the Centers for Disease Control (CDC) and the World Health Organization (WHO) amid a distorted view offered in a political context that caused many to question the validity of data. Who do schools trust in the political realities of what is safe or not became the question as decisions were made to open schools or not.

Dr. Steve Joel, superintendent of Lincoln Public Schools (LPS) located in Lincoln Nebraska, elaborated how key pivot points defined his work. The second largest public-school district in Nebraska, LPS serves 42,034 students supported by 3,300 teachers, 4,400 non-certified staff, and 300 school and system leaders. Dr. Joel has received numerous local, state, and national awards including the Nebraska Superintendent of the Year and Leadership Excellence by the Educational Resource Development Institute. LPS is a district that receives many acknowledgments over the course of a year and is regarded as a top urban district in the state and region.

Dr. Joel speaks to the inner tensions for school leaders as their leadership was tested by a crisis never experienced before in their tenure nor likely in the history of education. The complexities of decisions were driven by an unknown with changing information and a growing political division on how to keep schools open.

Stephen Joel, Ed.D.
Superintendent
Lincoln Public Schools
Lincoln, NE

When You Least Expect It...

If 27 years as a Superintendent has taught me one thing, it is to always expect the unexpected. Having had a number of experiences that tested my leadership resolve and plunged districts and communities I worked for into turmoil, I learned that to be effective and impactful I had to stick closely to my values as an educational leader. These "pivot" points have defined my work and I am proud of how we confronted and overcame challenges that had many with strong opinions.

But, the COVID-19 pandemic has been something else. In fact, I would argue that we have never experienced a crisis like this in the past nor will we ever again in most of our lives. More than just a virus to contend with, we are also faced with an economic recession, social unrest centered on Black Lives Matter, and, for an added stressor, a national election that could bring out the worst in some people. I had to become much more patient with people who held deeply different beliefs than I. For instance, at the beginning of our decision-making, I struggled with the "hoaxers" and "anti-maskers."

From the day I made the decision to call off school in March 2020, contrary to the strong recommendation of the Governor and Health Department to remain open, to one month before we are bringing students and staff back to an unknown school experience, this has been a summer

I nor any other school leader will ever forget. The most difficult lesson to remember is that any decision made will draw scrutiny and argument from others. But, these decisions are what we are paid to do.

There is no playbook for a pandemic so we had to develop one. This virus has been difficult to understand and the manner in which it has been portrayed in the media has made it hard to develop a "return to school" plan that people will accept. Fortunately for me, the Board of Education immediately granted me Emergency Powers to proceed without needing board approval. With this, my team and I were able to learn and act in a timely fashion. The work of the summer of 2020 yielded a 500+-page document that answers every question raised from staff, parents, and the community.

But, these efforts will clearly not be enough to satisfy the different sides of the debate. On one side we had been directed by the Governor and Commissioner of Education (May 2020) to develop plans to reopen and, on the other, we have been dealing with a formal staff protest that cites our inability to provide a safe environment in which there is no transmission of this insidious virus. The fear of some parents and staff has led to a remote learning option that will be synchronous and much more robust than what students experienced at the beginning of the pandemic.

The majority of my time this summer has been to make key decisions based on the best data we had at the time and to strengthen and support the resolve of our leaders and board members. It has been important that those in my office take the "heat" from the various emotional pleas so that our principals can focus on opening their schools. While we know this too shall pass, the concerns and anger that are directed at us today make the work more challenging but it remains the most important work we are committed to do.

As I look back at the last six months, I am again reminded about the importance of education and the necessity for leaders to step up and perform amazing tasks under difficult challenges. As in the past, I have witnessed people accomplish superhuman tasks in short timeframes because they knew they had to. Many of these leaders sacrificed personal and family time, and they can never be thanked enough. But that will be my ongoing focus and at the appropriate time when we can celebrate the end of the pandemic. This is a primary reason why we can never be correlated to a business—as we are a human enterprise. I stand proud of our work in the most trying of times.

I believe that most of our leadership lives are filled with joyous moments and accomplishments. It is inevitable, however, that there will be incredibly challenging and dark times that require each of us to lead through. These are lonely times that only colleagues understand, but these times will ultimately be replaced by relative normalcy.

Dr. Joel made clear that the impact of the COVID-19 pandemic has been like no other challenge amid numerous uncertainties and mounting distractions. The burden for leaders created lonely times, but he sees hope and opportunity ahead.

Distractions ensued from tweets from President Trump pressuring schools to open by downplaying imminent health risks. There were political threats to withhold funding and/or change funding criteria for school systems that would not open face-to-face for fall 2020 broke system efforts. Turbulence continued as city and state leaders clashed over policies about shuttering in place, opening of business establishments, implementing social distancing protocols, and wearing facial masks in public.

In spite of political actors at the state and federal levels, systems and leaders held resolve to do what was best for the safety and health of students and teachers. Backlash ensued from the public regardless of the configuration of school plans—ranging from face-to-face, fully remote, or a hybrid model. Teacher unions sued state governments (e.g., Florida), while parents and teachers voiced loudly concerns for a safe beginning of the year. Pockets of parents protested demanding a face-to-face return while other parents protested demanding only virtual learning options.

In August 2020, the voices of teachers were muted and became alienated from their professional expertise when the White House dubbed them as essential workers. This declaration made teachers obligated to return to school—regardless of their own health and safety issues. Vice-President Pence shared with state governors that "the administration has designated teachers as essential workers, but said it was not a mandate" (Westwood, 2020, para. 4). A concerned parent spoke to the quandary of the essential worker:

> Are teachers essential workers? Schools cannot open if too many teachers have COVID-19 or are quarantining because of exposure to it. For some political and district leaders, this means teachers should be designated essential workers, who could be required to work if they have the virus or have been exposed to it.
>
> Teachers are essential—any parent will attest to that. It is less clear what the effects of issuing this designation might be. Some teachers are comfortable with this label, but many others are not, particularly those with a high-risk medical condition. They worry that it will increase transmission of the virus.
>
> Imposing this label may erode trust between district leaders and teachers, creating or adding to a perception of "us vs. them," which could undermine teachers' commitment to the profession. However, district leaders move forward amidst the hard challenges of opening schools in a pandemic, creating meaningful dialogue and consistent transparency with teachers should not be an after-thought or an add-on. It should be embedded in their work.

Whereas Governor Ron DeSantis (Florida) ordered schools to reopen (later this decision was rescinded by court order), others begrudgingly provided systems latitude, as in the case of New York City Schools, only after the United Federation of Teachers threatened to strike. Governor Coumo referred to the opening of K-12 schools as the "canary in a coal mine" (Hallum, 2020, para. 2).

From the onset of the pandemic, the public watched as front-line spectators and actors, as social media in real-time fashion fueled involvement and engagement.

The Influence of Social Media

Superintendents and school leaders have the added responsibility of navigating the unknown as the pressures mount to balance the best safety decisions with the best education decisions. Social media allowed the world to experience the COVID-19 pandemic and provided an in-depth look at life in schools as leaders tried to make sense of the coronavirus's impact on students, teachers, parents, federal and state funding, and so much more. However, the large gush of perspectives including distortions made it difficult to wade through the rationales for decision-making.

Regardless of system context—urban, rural, suburban—the noise surrounding COVID-19 has been deafening to listen to through the amplified political grandstanding, finger-pointing, and identifying and separating educational leaders by their views and positions. Added to the noise was a hotly contested presidential election, something that is always preceded by media slanting and mudslinging with personal and professional nastiness. In a day of full-throttle media outlets without any controls, the storylines become even more contested, jaded, and ugly.

The positions taken by key leaders across the country reflect deep divides in positions with little overlapping agreements. To illustrate these points, the following are offered:

President Trump: After being questioned about the death toll of COVID-19, President Trump responded, "It is what it is" (Cole & Subramaniam, 2020, para 1).

The School Superintendents Association contends that the reopening of schools should be a local or regional decision informed by applicable health, safety, and disinfecting recommendations articulated by the Centers for Disease Control and Prevention, as well as state and local health agencies (AASA, 2020, para. 3).

Education Secretary DeVos: "School leaders across the country need to be making plans" to have students in the classroom, DeVos said. "There will be exceptions to the rule, but the rule should be kids go back to school this fall" (Smith, 2020a, para. 8).

Press Secretary McEnany: "When he says open, he means open in full, kids being able to attend each and every day in their school. *The science should not stand in the way of this*" (Smith, 2020b, para. 3).

American Federation of Teachers: AFT President Randi Weingarten said, "Our blueprint serves as a stark contrast to the conflicting guidance, bluster and lies of the Trump administration (AFT, n.d., para. 12).

Florida Governor DeSantis: "But I'm confident if you can do Home Depot, if you can do Walmart, if you can do these things, we absolutely can do the schools," said DeSantis. "I want our kids to be able to minimize this education gap that I think has developed" (Sullivan, 2020, para. 4).

National Education Association: "[A]nxious educators have a message for administrators and lawmakers: We want to teach our students, but we don't want to die doing it" (Flannery, 2020, para. 1).

Education leaders were challenged to fulfill their responsibilities in the face of the rants in social media and the injection of inaccurate data against the backdrop of the polarized positions made by state and federal leaders.

 ## New Trajectories

COVID-19 has and will continue to change education, altering the trajectory of the ways in which students learn, teachers teach, and leaders lead. In a virtual space, leaders needed to focus on trying to bring calm logic and coherence to the immediate disequilibrium. As the pandemic continued, school planning moved to the long term as leaders sought to find a new equilibrium to create stability and predictability. As we were writing this book, we spoke with many students, teachers, and parents and included their voices. They had a great deal to say.

Students are at the center of education with over 56 million in our nation's schools. A student's school experience had no greater disruption than that caused by COVID-19 and shutting the schoolhouse doors, disrupting the support they needed to grow and develop. Detailing isolation, a seventh-grade student shared:

> I am most worried about losing contact with my friends because last year we spent all day surrounded by people, but now I am spending 8–12 hours in my bedroom staring at a computer screen. While I do have Zooms all day, only ten people have their video on, we are on mute the whole time, and even in breakout rooms, there is no real chance to have a conversation or interact with the other kids. It's also just hard to go on with only texting someone for five minutes a day.

As a mother picked up her son the day the school had to shut down because of surge in COVID-19, the first-grader pleaded:

> I miss my friends. That was my friend Micha's classroom; he was across the hall from me. Why can't we go back in? They are still in there. I see the Flag.

I like the Flag. The flag is close to where my bus comes. "I WANT TO SEE MRS.
…! I MISS HER!"

A fourth-grade student paralleled the endurance it takes to climb a mountain and her experiences with school in fall 2020:

> When you're hiking on a mountain, sometimes it's fun and other times it feels overwhelming. That's what school is like in quarantine. Most days, it's on the overwhelming side. I would like it a lot more if we were face-to-face. I miss my friends and teachers.

A high school junior elaborated:

> These times of quarantine have been quite difficult for me to navigate as well as my friends. It has been unlike anything most of us have personally experienced. We all have our own views on what COVID-19 has done to our lives. For me, this whole situation has been very challenging to deal with especially in regards to participating in the marching band and cross-country team at my school. Being a student-athlete and involved with many extracurricular activities, this has taken a major toll on my "normal" life such as my social life and my ability to focus on school. There are so many things my friends and I are missing out on due to this pandemic like performing at our Friday football games and going to the school retreat offered only twice a year. We are not able to do anything as planned in terms of school activities, and we have to cope with learning everything online instead of in a productive classroom environment.

Succinctly, a third-grade student declared, "I felt weird, and I thought that school would never be the same again." Further complicating this new scenario was the uncertainties of the impact of COVID-19 from not only just closing schools and going virtual, but also to the risk of dying.

Teachers were hit with tremendous challenges when the routines that they were most familiar no longer existed. The ability to see and talk with their students in person changed the dynamics of student and teacher relationships. Daily routines such as planning morphed into a new virtual space with little preparation. Adding to the challenge was the need to balance their teaching responsibilities at school along with their own children's education. A fourth-grade teacher shared:

Framing Unprecedented Disruptions

> I've spent much of the pandemic wondering what personal risks I'm willing to accept as a teacher. When school shootings happened, I reassured myself by thinking, "It's not likely to happen to you. You'll be OK," and I'd hug the children who needed comforting after each traumatic lockdown drill.
>
> But I can't do that now.
>
> I'm teaching from a makeshift workspace in my bedroom while my husband juggles telework and connects our children to their online classrooms. Insomnia wrecks my nights as I worry about everything. We're told we might head back to the building soon, but my well-rehearsed narrative for handling the bad parts of this job won't work now. The risks are real, we might not be OK, and hugs aren't compatible with social distancing.
>
> I can't let myself become a martyr in the classroom, but my heart will break if I walk away. I need new boundaries.

The stress to make significant shifts in their pedagogy combined with the stress caused by not being able to meet the needs of their students wore heavily on teachers. The social emotional drain became more apparent as school doors remained closed.

As schools made plans to open, teachers observed that their health and welfare was not a priority. A middle school teacher made these observations:

> I love my vocation and looked forward to safely returning to the classroom, assuming we'd follow successful European models and be protected at the level of basic health care workers. However, our district, like many, proceeded with "masks suggested." One in 20 students wear a mask. I planned to teach behind a plastic sheet. However, when the first head popped up with a puzzled look, it was impossible not to circulate among my students. I sanitize where I can, but each day I leave with a feeling of dread. I am sad our superintendents and leaders abandoned the safety of teachers and students, ignoring science and caving to a misguided political will. Walmart and Target care for their employees more.

It has been predicted that 20% of the teaching force will leave the profession permanently, and many others will rely on other protections to not return physically to their schools. The health of teachers and their resistance to return quickly emerged as another priority.

Parents were thrust into making decisions and compromises as they balanced the safety and education of their children with their need to

Framing Unprecedented Disruptions

work and generate income to support them. The impact of COVID-19 was not isolated to education as parents either lost their jobs or in many situations, transitioned to a virtual environment requiring change similar to the experiences of teachers and students. A parent related, "The system is not working. Mothers, fathers, siblings, and grandparents are attempting to navigate a maddening system with which we have no map to guide us." This parent continued:

> In March 2019, I was working full-time. Our son was thriving in kindergarten. In the blink of an eye, I became a stay-at-home-mom. I had no clue what I was doing. Virtual learning was a mess. I met with our son's teacher after the school year ended. She hinted that it was "all a joke." The test scores had been "frozen" since schools closed, and all the hard work we had put in at home didn't matter. Ouch.
>
> Our son misses his friends and teachers. Explaining COVID-19 to a six, now seven-year-old is impossible. (Wear your mask, don't touch anyone, wash your hands for 20 seconds, six feet apart).
>
> Our county was unclear about plans for schools to reopen. Virtual learning plans were well laid but sadly, one week before school was to "Open," our Superintendent changed the "Schedule." Parents were instructed to select, for a third time, which solution was best for their child. We selected "Virtual Learning" over "F2F Learning." (I know, I'm confused too.)
>
> Moving forward I feel the school districts should NOT waiver on decisions. I believe schools should offer counseling to students as well as their caregivers. Our public education system is crumbling and our children are suffering for it.

Emerging from this short-term alteration to daily learning was the revelation of the importance of the many functions connected to educating children. Providing special services for students with unique needs immediately became a concern. A parent indicated:

> I am a mother of two daughters: a typically developing 16-year old and a special needs (Deaf/Hard-of-Hearing) 13-year-old. Parenting each in their education during COVID-19 has been two different experiences.
>
> Due to the rapid changes occurring in March with shelter in place, teaching changed on a dime and it became difficult to meet my students' needs. There was no set schedule nor was there one standard place for students to find texts, or assignments. Each teacher quickly was forced to

19

develop an augmented teaching style and use whatever online learning systems they chose. As a parent, assisting my students where to find their daily lessons was a challenge because of no uniformity. Both students could go a full week without direct contact from a teacher. There was zero contact with peers in any meaningful way. Online connections don't replace in person relationships.

My 16-year-old is self-driven and motivated. She has adapted well to changing education. My 13-year-old is a Deaf/Hard-of-Hearing individual and has accommodations through an IEP consisting primarily of accommodation in the classroom to level the playing field with her peers in hearing-related learning and issues. Remote learning under COVID-19 restrictions posed multiple challenges for her.

Parents and students faced numerous challenges with technology. A father of two children shared a poignant and doable perspective about what he wishes systems leaders would consider:

We benefit, today, from a world in which technology allowed school districts to pivot to remote learning. However, I think that the school districts should have better addressed a strategy to mitigate some of the negative aspects of technology which present subsequent problems as a result of its use. I think that the primary issues our children and families experienced included:

- social isolation from their peers;
- the negative impact of emotional and mental health due to long hours of exposure in front of an electronic screen (Shifrin et al., 2015); and,
- the challenge of working parents to assist their children in Internet and connectivity matters as well as providing supervision for children who are too young to be home alone.

The parents of two high school students shared not only their concerns about remote learning but also the hope that their children will be more resilient:

We are the parents of two very bright teenagers. We have a sophomore as well as a senior. The shutting down of our school due to the COVID-19 pandemic is one that has brought many issues into our lives. Of course, we fear for our children's safety as well as all of the teachers and staff, but we also

Framing Unprecedented Disruptions

fear for their futures. Our senior has not taken an ACT or a SAT and is missing crucial in-person learning. School is also a social outlet for these teens. Since the shutdown, our sophomore has isolated herself and primarily stays in her room. Last year, she was a thriving freshman ready to take on the world. This year, she is a shell of herself that does not do well with remote learning. Thankfully, our senior does not appear to have any problems, but he is missing college visits and all that senior year has to offer.

Yes, we understand the need for remote learning in the midst of this pandemic and the real possibility that this will continue far longer than we wish. We do not have the answers, but we do know that our children are facing an uphill climb for their future. This just might make them more resilient and better equipped to handle the world. We can only sit back and see what their future holds.

The voices of students, teachers, and parents offer leaders much to think about as systems respond to the unknowns of moving forward.

Leading for Tomorrow

We must be able to unpack and then address how education, the fundamental core of this nation, emerges stronger and more impactful for students. Moving forward, some of the most significant questions requiring new thinking must be addressed:

- How will schools respond to the care students need now and in the future? (Chapter 2)
- What is being learned during this time of shifting programs that will be carried forward in creating a new normal? (Chapter 3)
- How will the value of traditional conventions such as high-stakes testing change moving forward? (Chapter 4)
- What challenges will schools face in addressing the emergence of social and emotional stress? (Chapter 5)
- How will schools and community agencies return to a place that will likely no longer exist as it did pre-COVID-19? (Chapter 6)
- What are the challenging leadership realities as schools emerge from the COVID-19 pandemic? (Chapter 7)

These are some of the many questions pondered during this time of disruption as we researched the responses from districts across the country and analyzed the voices from educational leaders found in the chapter Narratives.

References

American Association of School Administrators. (2020, May 29). Resolution in support of a safe, healthy, and district-specific reopening process informed by the centers for disease control and prevention guidelines. *AASA Central*. http://aasacentral.org/wp-content/uploads/2020/05/AASA-Resolution-in-Support-of-a-Safe-Healthy-and-District-Specific-Reopening-Process.pdf

American Federation of Teachers. (n.d.). Safely reopening America's schools and communities. *AFT*. www.aft.org/reopen-schools

Cole, D., & Subramaniam, T. (2020, September 3). Trump on Covid death toll: "It is what it is." *CNN*. www.cnn.com/2020/08/04/politics/trump-covid-death-toll-is-what-it-is/index.html

Committee on Education & Labor. (2020). Coronavirus Aid, Relief, and Economic Security (CARES) Act: Education provisions. *EdLabor House*. https://edlabor.house.gov/imo/media/doc/2020-03-31%20CARES%20Act%20Education%20Fact%20Sheet[2].pdf

Couros, G. (2020, April 15). "… we are all isolated across the entire world together." *George Couros*. https://georgecouros.ca/blog/archives/11608

Flannery, M. E. (2020, July 22). Educators prepare for reopening with living wills and life insurance. *NeaToday*. http://neatoday.org/2020/07/22/educators-speak-out-on-reopening-schools-safely/?_ga=2.151820539.393330258.1595955085-917570839.1592328324

Hallum, M. (2020, August 30). COVID-19 outbreak at upstate SUNY campus 'canary in the coal mine' for schools reopening: Cuomo. *AMNY*. www.amny.com/education-2/covid-19-outbreak-at-upstate-suny-campus-canary-in-the-coal-mine-for-schools-reopening-cuomo/

Magee, M. P. (2020, April 5). The new reality roundup: Week 4. *50Can*. https://50can.org/blog/the-new-reality-roundup-week-4/

Shifrin, D., Brown, A., Hill, D., Laura, J., & Flinn, S. K. (2015). Growing up digital: Media research symposium. *American Academy of Pediatrics*. www.aap.org/en-us/Documents/digital_media_symposium_proceedings.pdf

Smith, A. (2020a, July 12). DeVos defends push to reopen schools as Trump administration is accused of "messing with" children's health. *NBCNews*. www.nbcnews.com/politics/donald-trump/devos-defends-push-reopen-schools-trump-admin-accused-messing-children-n1233601

Smith, A. (2020b, July 16). White House press secretary: "The science should not stand in the way of" schools fully reopening. *NBCNews*. www.nbcnews.com/politics/donald-trump/white-house-press-secretary-science-should-not-stand-way-schools-n1234102

Sullivan, K. (2020, July 10). Florida Gov. DeSantis says schools can open if Walmart and Home Depot are open. *CNN*. www.cnn.com/2020/07/10/politics/florida-desantis-walmart-home-depot-schools-reopen/index.html

Westwood, S. (2020, August 21). White House formally declaring teachers essential workers. *CNN*. www.cnn.com/2020/08/20/politics/white-house-teachers-essential-workers/index.html

Wheatley, M. (2003). When change is out of our control. In M. Effron, R. Gandossy, & M. Goldsmith (Eds.), *Human resources in the 21st century*. Wiley.

Teachers and Leaders Care First for Their Students

2

In This Chapter...

Introduction	24
The Absence of Traditional School Structures	25
Narrative: *You Are Not Alone*	26
Parents Assume Different Roles	34
Narrative: *Supporting Parents and Caregivers During Uncertain and Disruptive Times*	35
Meeting the Unique Needs of Children	38
Narrative: *Learning to Work with Tools from a New Toolbox: Student Supports During COVID-19*	42
Leading for Tomorrow	45
References	46

Introduction

There were many heroes in the midst of the COVID-19 pandemic as every sector of society reached out to their communities during this crisis. Our superheroes in education are teachers and school leaders. The country finally saw the importance of what teachers do every day as well as feel that weight of responsibility. Social media provided public insight into how teachers and leaders made heroic efforts to provide safety-nets for students

Teachers, Leaders Care First for Students

and parents who were distanced from schools. Examined in this chapter is the impact of eliminating traditional school structures, the different roles parents assumed, and the new systems to meet the unique needs of children.

The Absence of Traditional School Structures

Moving to a virtual environment practically happened overnight, changing the traditional school structures across the country for more than 56 million students. The normal routines from stepping on the bus in the morning to attending after-school activities such as athletics and drama ceased to exist for almost all students sometime in April 2020. Nonetheless, through extraordinary efforts, creative approaches were created to preserve and adapt fundamental structures of schools including daily schedules and routines.

Rituals and Routines

Throughout the pandemic, the rituals and routines familiar to schools across America such as bus pickups, classroom bells, class periods, lunchtime, and after-school activities ceased immediately. For teachers, common planning time moved to preparing for teaching in a virtual environment. Leaders fast-paced the acquisition of mobile devices and put in place multiple options so students could connect with their teachers online.

Keeping students connected to the classroom became a priority and most districts redesigned their technology plans to put a device in the hands of every student and scurried to find new ways to ensure access to the Internet. Teachers created new online lessons and developed daily schedules to connect with students via a virtual environment. In an interview with John Bosselman, Director of Instruction at Latitude High School (Oakland, California), Fasso (2020) reported that in a virtual environment it is essential to "keep a daily rhythm and rituals that allow for students to be in discussion and collaboration with each other, including regular communication protocols" (para. 8).

Although teachers and leaders went to great lengths to stay connected with their students, some students fell through the cyber cracks when

25

the schoolhouse doors shut. For example, State Superintendent Molly Spearman of South Carolina told a panel of leaders that she "estimates between 4% and 5% of students or about 31,000 to 39,000 have been unaccounted for since public schools closed" (Gilreath, 2020, para. 5). In a needs assessment of the 178 school districts in Colorado, an estimated 55,000 students did not have access to a Wi-Fi-enabled device and about 64,000 students did not have access to the Internet (Breunlin, 2020).

Staying connected to students, teachers, and the community was a top priority for Dr. Grant Rivera, superintendent of Marietta City Schools (MCS), located in Marietta, Georgia. MCS serves 9,721 students supported by 659 teachers and 161 certified personnel. Prior to leading Marietta City Schools, Dr. Rivera served as the Chief of Staff for the Cobb County School District. He has also served as a high school principal, assistant principal, special education teacher, and coach in the Cobb County School District. During his tenure in Marietta, student achievement has increased across every student cohort, including students identified as Black, Hispanic, Students with Disabilities, and English Learners. Additionally, the district established both a Pre-K Early Learning Center and a College and Career Academy.

In his Narrative, Dr. Rivera describes how COVID-19's unpredictability led to a need for predictability and stability in his district. His primary role in the system and the Marietta community was to stay connected with students and their parents through continuous communication and compassion.

Grant Rivera, Ed.D.
Superintendent
Marietta City Schools
Marietta, GA

You Are Not Alone

We are experiencing an academic pandemic. Equally relevant, COVID-19 created a pandemic of social isolation for our students. As we deal with the realities of learning loss, we must also be responsive to how isolation has negatively impacted our students' sense of community. Relationships matter, especially during this dual pandemic.

To that end, despite the unfortunate reality that our classrooms were dark and our schools were locked during this pandemic, Marietta City Schools created strategic opportunities for students to experience a sense of belonging and personal accountability. Our intention was to show our children that they were more than a test score. Our children are valued members of this Marietta family and their safety, stability, and nutrition were important to our 1,400-plus staff members and the larger community we serve.

Academic Connectedness and Accountability

Perhaps the greatest tragedy of virtual learning is when a student disappears. A child with a face, name, and performance during in-person learning who, in the transition to the virtual space, never reconnects to their teacher or classmates caused us great alarm. Our educators were not prepared or equipped to respond to this type of disappearance. Truth be told, in the days and weeks that followed school closures, many educators were satisfied with the most basic level of self-survival. Success was now defined by the heroic efforts of building an online curriculum within days while simultaneously trying to teach, Zoom, and manage their own family dynamics (because let's face it... the educator's kid wasn't in school either). In all the madness, students could easily disappear from a computer screen, losing all sense of connectedness. And let's be fair—what could we really expect teachers to do about this disappearance (proactively or reactively) while they taught class from the confines of their own living or dining room?

A Three-layered Approach

In Marietta, we created a layered approach to personal student accountability and connectedness that engaged numerous staff members, both in-person and virtually:

- Each Monday during virtual learning, student engagement data from our learning management system (Schoology) were analyzed by central office staff in an effort to batch all students into one of three categories: high engagement, low engagement, or no engagement. Student engagement was defined as the degree to which students were logging into Schoology and engaging with class lessons and assignments.

- Each school established an intervention team that would contact the family of each student showing low or no engagement in virtual learning. The staff member would identify the root cause for the student's disengagement and virtual disappearance, and then provide whatever resources necessary to re-engage both the child and the family in learning.

- Through personal relationships and shared accountability (including an occasional home visit), our students and their families quickly learned their virtual presence mattered. They knew we would come calling or knocking if we consistently did not see their faces on a computer screen or their engagement in learning. This same type of accountability, commonly known as compulsory school attendance, was in place for in-person learning during the "normal" school year so why would we not do the same for virtual learning?

Family Resources

Each week, as our school intervention teams were having personal conversations with the children falling behind due to COVID-19, we developed a community root-cause analysis for why students and families were unable to connect to learning and, subsequently, maintain meaningful relationships with their teachers and their classmates. This analysis was critically important in our efforts to proactively support our students and to anticipate their needs before they became statistics.

Proactive Responses

The phone calls, text messages, emails, and home visits revealed consistent dynamics as to why a child would be personally and academically alienated:

- **Food insecurity:** Students can't learn well if they don't eat well. Our response—over 7,000 meals per day were delivered in our community at 81 different bus stops along 19 different bus routes five days a week throughout the school closure.

- **Technology:** Students can't virtually engage in learning without a device. Our response—we distributed over 3,300 Chromebooks to students in the first three weeks of virtual learning. Additionally, we tailored devices to the age of the child, as demonstrated by the 57 tablets provided to our preK learners that allowed for easier functionality than a traditional laptop.

- **Internet:** Students can't consistently learn without consistent connectivity. Our response—over 1,000 personal Wi-Fi hotspots were provided to families to address connectivity issues, particularly for our lower-income families. Wi-Fi-enabled school buses were also strategically placed throughout the community in densely populated areas such as apartment complexes, allowing more than 300 students per day to have additional access to the Internet.

Ultimately, we can track our degree of success in proactively providing each student and family with resources and support. The collective efforts of this village we call Marietta were able to achieve an exceptionally high rate of student engagement during the school closure in that 97% of all preK through 12th-grade students virtually engaged with their teachers between March and May 2020.

This success wasn't luck, it was learning; it wasn't chance, it was connectedness.

Communication
As we navigated the personal and academic trauma that resulted from COVID-19 and virtual learning, we acknowledged the importance of *overcommunicating* with our families. As leaders, we could not provide certainty; however, we could provide clarity. It became critically important that we bring our families along in the process through a high-degree of communication. To that end, we developed strategic communication that encompassed consistent values and action items:

- **Family guides:** With every pivot from virtual to in-person to hybrid learning models, our families would receive a comprehensive family guide at the time of the district-wide announcement. This document included a variety of academic and operational considerations (written from a family perspective) about the current phase of learning.

Our priority was to never make a major decision that left parents wondering how that would impact their child and family dynamics.

Teachers, Leaders Care First for Students

- **Town halls:** We conducted 52 interactive but different community town halls at various phases of school closure and during our deliberations about reopening. These sessions were recorded and intentionally formatted to reach the diverse needs of our community. For example, some sessions were grouped by level (elementary, middle, and high); others by language (English and Spanish); others by program (families of students with disabilities or families of English Language Learners).

- **Surveys:** We kept a pulse on our system to determine what we could do better by distributing surveys to families at key times. We needed to know what was working well and what needed to improve. Our surveys were offered on-line in both English and Spanish. The results of these surveys helped to shape our thinking and actions as we moved through COVID-19.

Our plan was simple: communicate early, often, and with a high degree of transparency. The whiplash of the COVID-19 roller-coaster on schooling and, subsequently, family dynamics may have been unavoidable; however, I would argue that the communication part of the ride was within our control. For our system, it was critically important that our communication approach was slow, steady, and predictable.

Regardless of the ever-present and changing dynamics of COVID-19, Dr. Rivera's key to navigating the pandemic was creating two-way communication streams to build a community of responsiveness, illustrating that educating students is a human endeavor no matter the situation or setting.

Teaching and Learning is a Human Endeavor

Schools had to do more than just patch classroom routines and course content. Teachers, counselors, social workers, and leaders had to meet other more pressing basic needs of their students. Within days, federal and state programs such as free and reduced meals continued as cafeteria

Teachers, Leaders Care First for Students

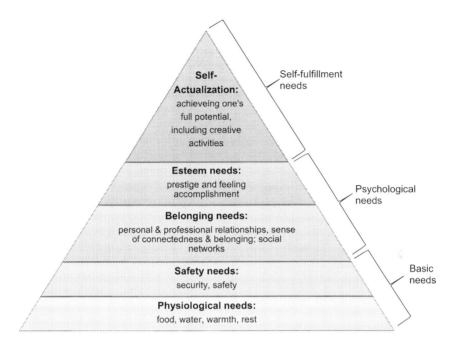

Figure 2.1 Maslow's Hierarchy of Needs
Adapted from McLeod (2020) and Maslow (1943).

workers and volunteers packaged breakfasts and lunches, and delivered them to community spots. Figure 2.1 illustrates Maslow's Hierarchy of Needs (1943).

Primal in the pyramid of needs is a sense of security and belonging which required an immediate response from schools. Teachers and principals understood the importance of student relationships and found new ways to stay connected with them. Whether driving by their homes and waving good morning and shouting hello from their cars or creating virtual opportunities to see and talk with their students, the need to stay connected while keeping them safe was a priority.

Developing positive relationships is bedrock for student development and learning. While a child's development is shaped by many factors outside of school, interactions in a classroom are critical to social development and academic performance. The COVID-19 pandemic significantly impacted the needed interactions provided by teachers in their classrooms. The changes in school structures, the disruptions to schedules, and the fears about COVID-19 brought to bear a greater importance for staying connected with students to reassure them of their safety and to minimize the trauma that each may be experiencing.

Disparities, Equal Access, and Achievement Gaps

The issues surrounding equity in education have always been part of the conversations about improving student outcomes. Disparities impacting education exist across income, race, gender, language, ethnicity, geographic location, etc. With the COVID-19 pandemic and schools moving to virtual environments, Rothstein (2020) predicted that "existing academic achievement differences between middle-class and low-income students will explode" (para. 1). Factors that will have the greatest impact include (Strauss, 2020):

1. White-collar parents who work from home and support their children vs. many low-income parents who are required to work outside the home.
2. Lack of access to the Internet and devices for low-income and rural families with a greater impact on minority families.
3. The ability for parents to support their children's school based on their own education level.
4. The impact of stress resulting from crowded living conditions.
5. Incidents of physical and psychological abuse.

Even though schools have struggled, they are the primary source for providing additional support to close learning gaps by meeting the unique needs of students.

In efforts to ensure equal access in a totally digital environment, districts through state and federal support were able to procure a large number of digital devices and Internet access for students and families. Furthermore, systems became creative in Internet connectivity through the use of mobile hotspots, Internet on buses parked in neighborhoods, and collaboration with businesses.

For many community members, it was the first time they recognized the value and the priority to connect children and families to the Internet. However, for pockets across systems, the access divide became apparent, and "Even in the best-resourced and highest-performing education systems, most COVID responses in education will end up by privileging better-off children" (Mundy & Hares, 2020, para. 2). In a Gallup poll, 52% of nonwhite parents indicated a concern while 36% of white parents expressed concern (Brenan, 2020).

When schools moved to online virtual environments, equity questions quickly emerged around access, given that more than nine million children could not connect to the Internet (USAFacts, 2020). Stark contrasts and disparities became more apparent between students that come from privileged households and students that come from poverty households. Students that lacked strong home support and Internet connectivity were further challenged and this widened the learning gaps that already existed

The achievement gap widened and included students not only disconnected due to a lack of Internet access but also included a growing number of students who either chose not to do the work online or who struggled with online learning. Educators reported that students with resources were struggling due to lack of focus at home and lower-income students did not get the needed support at home, further compounding inequities (Jarrett & Pomrenze, 2020).

Addressing achievement gaps will require new resources as well as flexibility in how current resources can be leveraged within accountability metrics. The Coronavirus Aid, Relief, and Economic Security (CARES) Act (2020) was passed to provide additional resources to states for district distribution and to give more local discretion to modify the uses of existing Federal Title funds. Even with Federal support, the fiscal challenges from the economic slowdown will create greater disparities in school funding, further widening the gaps in needed student support.

Adding to the challenges schools face in the online shift will be a focus for schools to address learning loss on top of an already existing learning gap. Preliminary COVID-19 slide estimates that some students returning in the fall of 2020 will experience a full year of academic loss, requiring districts to determine how to approach these learning gaps and losses (Kuhfeld & Tarasawa, 2020).

Parents Assume Different Roles

Without much doubt, one of the largest shifts and challenges during COVID-19 was changing the role of parents. Alongside their responsibilities as parents, they were thrust into roles such as instructional assistant, tutor, playground aid, and full-time teacher.

Parents as Teachers

Although students and their teachers could make connections at home during the day through a range of media tools, the bottom line was that parents needed to be present and involved especially with children in lower grades. While parents accepted this role as best as they could, more than 91% of parents polled in New York expressed concerns about their children falling behind, ranking this higher than finance or socioemotional concerns (Education Trust-New York, 2020).

The support parents provided their children varied greatly and was often influenced by their ability to be at home during the school day, their access to the Internet, and the instructional delivery system provided by their schools. While some parents had flexibility as their workplaces shifted to home, others were required to leave home for the workplace, needing to find ways to supervise their children or enroll them in childcare. Others needed to leave their homes to get Internet access or meals at centralized locations for their children. Teachers who were also parents had to split their home responsibility with their work, often with 200 students plus their own children. The strain on parents took its toll as many reported they were tired and frustrated (Bloch, 2020).

Parent Support and Balance

The balance between work and taking care of their families pushed parents to a maximum load. They were wearing out in their struggle to fulfill their multiple roles while at the same time acquiring new skills in teaching their children. Given the surge in COVID-19, numerous school systems remained virtual in fall 2020, delaying the implementation of an in-school hybrid model. These new parenting responsibilities did not become easier over time; therefore, parents needed to pay attention to their own physical, emotional, and mental well-being, and they needed to understand that doing so was not selfish but rather essential self-care (Zerotothree, 2020).

Support and balance for parents and caretakers are examined by Dr. Katherine Kelbaugh, the Executive Director of the Museum School of Avondale Estates located in Decatur, Georgia. She has been a teacher, assistant principal, and principal. Dr. Kelbaugh has been recognized for her work in education with the 2019 Georgia Charter School Leader of the Year award and the Atlanta Families' Principal's Excellence in Education award in 2015.

Dr. Kelbaugh provided perspective about the transitions and processes employed to support parents and caregivers as they shouldered these new roles with their children.

Katherine Kelbaugh, Ph.D.
Executive Director
Museum School of Avondale Estates
Decatur, Georgia

Supporting Parents and Caregivers During Uncertain and Disruptive Times

The Museum School of Avondale Estates is a grassroots, start-up K-8 charter school in metro Atlanta, serving close to 600 students supported by 90 full-time and part-time staff members. Our mission, *to inspire students, teachers, and the community to collaborate to develop strong critical thinking, interpersonal, and academic skills in our students, which will prepare them for real-world success*, serves as the compass when making decisions and creating policies. Additionally, our core values of respect, responsibility, cooperation, creativity, kindness, and sustainability drive school-level and board-level policy-making. The Museum School's response to the COVID-19 pandemic was no different. Decisions were backed specifically by the values of cooperation, responsibility, and kindness, and our commitment to preparing students for real-world success by collaborating with our school community.

The school's virtual learning approach and parent/caregiver support evolved throughout the pandemic. Original ideas and plans required adapting and tweaking once actually put into action with students and families. We adjusted based on the formal and informal feedback we received from parents, students, and staff through multiple surveys. Survey topics ranged from experiences with instructional plans to preferences for reopening and related policies. Just as effective schools respond to academic data, we analyzed our stakeholder feedback and implemented action steps based on the data.

Throughout the pandemic, our school prioritized regular, consistent communication. Traditional weekly newsletters transitioned to daily updates that included specific tips, resources, and reminders related to our school's plan for closure and virtual learning. Later, extensive instructional plans, a comprehensive guidebook for reopening the school, several Town Hall meetings, and a constantly updated COVID-19 webpage also ensured that our parents were current with school plans.

Our communication plan during the pandemic was guided by several key principles:

- **Be transparent:** We dedicated ourselves to honesty and transparency in our parent communication. We were not afraid to expose our vulnerability and express our uncertainty as we responded to the numerous challenges associated with the pandemic.
- **Communicate everything:** When we didn't have answers, we communicated to our parents/caregivers that we just didn't have answers yet. Additionally, when unveiling tough decisions, we provided justification so that our stakeholders had a clear understanding of the rationale behind challenging decisions and policies.

Frequent, comprehensive communication ensured that stakeholders had a good understanding of the school's plans and decisions, which was critical in a time of so many other questions and unknowns.

As we created virtual learning plans in the spring, and then revised them in the fall, we acknowledged the significant role our parents/caregivers play in executing these plans. We made it a priority to understand and respond to these needs through:

Teachers, Leaders Care First for Students

- Implementation of a flex day, once a week, at which time students could catch up on assignments or engage in remediation or enrichment activities.
- Daily communication with helpful tips and reminders for a successful virtual learning experience.
- Material distribution of Chromebooks, hotspots, supplemental workbooks, school supplies, grocery gift cards, and meals and snacks for families in need.
- Strategies and resources for extending "bubbles" and/or creating quarantine pods with other families for social/emotional, academic, or child care purposes.

Family and support remained a top focus area for school leadership and staff throughout the pandemic.

Just as our society as a whole will never fully go back to the way things were before, neither will K-12 parents. However, this may not be all bad. Parents/caregivers are even more involved now; they have a deeper understanding of their child's academic, behavioral, and social needs, which may include a mixture of celebrations and gaps. Parents may be asking questions they have never thought of before. Is my child being challenged enough? Is this work too hard? Why is my child not able to work independently?

Parents' "new" knowledge will likely lead to more engagement and involvement with their child's education. Schools should be prepared for parents to ask more questions, demand more accommodations, and insist on learning environments that best meet their child's needs. More than ever, parents will advocate to ensure their child has the most positive, fulfilling, and productive educational experience possible. Whether it is realizing a particular environment in which their child works best or certain circumstances under which their child thrives, parents/caregivers should take advantage of this new knowledge.

As we look to the future, we undoubtedly will face other moments of disruption and turbulence, whether it is a natural disaster, an unexpected crisis, or a global pandemic. And as educators, we are going to once again be called upon to provide stability, comfort, and strength to adolescents and the community at large. Others have learned during this pandemic what we as educators have always known; education and schools are the nucleus of the community. As we prepare to once again face crises, here are a few insights for schools and districts:

- Carry forward your mission, especially when facing turbulence. Let your mission and core values guide your work. Your commitment to your mission should be evident in your policies, decisions, processes, budget, and overall communication to stakeholders.
- Expect decisions, policies, and reactions to evolve. Ideas supported by staff and parents early in a crisis may change as community and personal circumstances change. Seek feedback frequently and prepare to respond differently throughout the crisis.
- Reflect and debrief often during the crisis. How can we make these new policies and procedures even more effective now? Looking ahead, how can some of these new policies increase effectiveness and positive outcomes even in normal, traditional times?

In summary, during the COVID-19 pandemic, schools and districts across the country, supported parents and caregivers along with students and staff. Through frequent, honest communication and a commitment to listening to families, schools and districts can create partnerships with parents that prioritize student needs, even in times of disruption. As we look to the future, schools should prepare for and embrace parents' new role as informed advocates for their children. And with an eye towards the future, educators should reflect now and take note of current experiences that could lead to thoughtful, meaningful policies later.

Dr. Kelbaugh described the support parents needed both in the new role in educating their children and in the support needed to balance their own lives.

Meeting the Unique Needs of Children

The COVID-19 outbreak heightened awareness of the school's responsibilities to meet the needs of unique populations including those with

Individual Education Plans (IEPs) and Section 504 plans, for example. The virtual environment presented challenges to meeting these needs as well as adjusting approaches to meet the social emotional needs of students.

Gaps and Challenges

When schools moved online, many of the services students were entitled to disappeared. While some of the supports were critical to a student's well-being and learning, they were not required under the law. Other supports were legally required and had to adhere to strict procedures, such as Individualized Learning Plans (IEPs). Students whose unique needs were defined and regulated under the law required new approaches for support.

Through the online environment, the requirements of IEPs have been difficult to implement and this is of great concern for parents, special education teachers, and advocates. Experts predict substantive learning losses for special education students and that additional learning supports would be required that were not needed before COVID-19. In addition, schools will likely need to provide compensatory services to address learning loss once they return to school (Jacobson, 2020).

Schools needed to address the social emotional impact on students as well, reporting cases of physical and emotional abuse at home. The sexual abuse hotline RAINN saw a 22% increase in monthly calls to its hotline calls during the March 2020 lockdown—a record high (Kamenetz, 2020). Lindsey Jensen, a 2018 Teacher of the Year (Illinois), articulates what she fears:

> What currently keeps me up at night is the thought that too many students are living in abuse and neglect. What keeps me up at night is the thought of our LGBTQ+ students who are living in homes where they aren't accepted for who they are. What keeps me up at night are our students who don't have access to basic needs, such as food.
>
> (Walker, 2020, para. 19)

In moving to virtual environments, schools needed to develop new processes to meet their legal responsibilities.

Legal Responsibilities

The legal guidance for educational requirements such as special education and Section 504 are guided by federal interpretation. Although COVID-19 has presented numerous challenges, it does not allow local education agencies (LEAs) to compromise the access of a student with special needs to a free and appropriate public education (FAPE). If an LEA closes for a period of time and does not offer any instructional service to the general student population, then services are not required for students with an IEP under FAPE. However, students with individual education plans (IEPs) must have appropriate accommodations if schools are in session and other students are receiving an education (Gavin, 2020). When schools offered instruction through an online environment to the general student population, then LEAs were required to meet the conditions outlined in a student's IEP.

Schools are mandated reporters of child abuse. The federal government through the Federal Child Abuse Prevention and Legal Treatment Act (CAPTA) (2010) establishes the minimum standards required for states to receive Federal dollars. With school districts moving to a virtual model, states have seen up to a 50% decrease in school reporting, creating strong concerns about the safety of students.

Student Services in a Virtual Environment

Schools were challenged to provide student services that were typically provided in person (Gao & Hill, 2020). Federal guidance for schools during COVID-19 outlined that a student's "team may, but are not required to, include distance learning plans in a child's IEP that could be triggered and implemented during a selective closure due to a COVID-19 outbreak" (Department of Education, 2020, p. 5). With regard to providing services in a virtual environment, schools may provide services "at an alternate location or the provision of online or virtual instruction, instructional telephone calls, and other curriculum-based instructional activities, and may identify which special education and related services, if any, could be provided at the child's home" (Department of Education, 2020, p. 5).

While schools squeaked flexibility in by providing services through online instructional designs, special education advocates were concerned that waivers could impact a student's civil rights and moreover, not be adequate in meeting their needs under IDEA (Modan, 2020). As school personnel develop and make changes associated with online learning environments, they must be prepared for legal action from parents and advocates in meeting the accommodations set forth in IEPs. Moreover, schools may likely be required to provide compensatory support for services not provided when students return to school, post-COVID-19 (Jacobson, 2020).

Digital advocates portray a different version of technology to meet student accommodations. Virtual public schools use an online environment with a variety of tools to not only personalize instruction but also to make accommodations in meeting the learning needs of special education students (Collopy, 2020). Accommodations could include virtual meetings, the use of verbal and visual prompts and cues, etc. The success of meeting the special needs of children through a virtual environment requires extensive professional learning. Unfortunately, most schools were not prepared to provide services in this format and even with rapid and short-term professional learning, teachers were not adequately prepared to provide the strategies students require.

Recognizing the need for response to the unique needs of students in a virtual environment, Dr. Dawn Meyers, the Social Emotional Learning Specialist at Foothills Education Charter High School (Athens, GA), examines in her Narrative some new tools to support students. Foothills Education Charter High School is a Georgia public State Charter Commission School affirmed by the Georgia Department of Education. Opened in 2015, Foothills serves nearly 2,000 students at 17 (soon to be 19) individual sites in partner school districts, Georgia Department of Corrections locations, and a virtual Youth Challenge site serving Ft. Gordon and Ft. Stewart. Foothills is a second-chance resource that offers students an opportunity to earn a high school diploma.

As schools shut their doors and moved teaching and learning into family homes, the human element of schools, which is foundational to social development, changed dramatically. Dr. Meyers, through her experience in working with diverse families, understood what families were facing and saw opportunities in how family service could be strengthened by what was learned during this pandemic.

Dawn Meyers, Ed.D.
Social Emotional Learning Specialist
Foothills Education Charter High School
Athens, GA

Learning to Work with Tools from a New Toolbox: Student Supports During COVID-19

The abrupt COVID-19 school closures during the spring of 2020 forced everyone working in schools to operate differently. Teachers pivoted to teach virtually, bus drivers delivered meals to neighborhoods instead of transporting children to and from school, and student support service professionals adapted their practices to serve students and families. There were positive impacts of school closures and social distancing. It's ironic that the same virus that pulled us apart physically made us work more closely together. As some of the prototypical tools used by student support school professionals seemingly disappeared overnight, we were forced to fill the gap with new tools to reach students—and so, a new toolbox was created.

New Tools in the Toolbox

School nurses, school social workers, school counselors, school psychologists, graduation coaches, and those serving special populations such as migrant specialists and homeless liaisons were cast into center stage roles. The inextricable link between social emotional health and wellness and academic success has long been acknowledged. However, in the midst of a global pandemic, families, schools and communities collectively felt the effects of the importance of basic needs ahead of learning as concerns over food insecurity, anxiety and depression, and physical illness became paramount to learning. Student support staff either adapted their tools or created new ones to address these concerns in the changed school environment.

One example of a new tool or skills is how student support professionals became consultants in partnership with other adults (parents and guardians) instead of direct service providers to children. School nurses, accustomed to managing students with chronic illness during the school day, spent hours on the telephone helping to manage refilling prescriptions or obtaining diabetes supplies and nebulizers. Nurses also became translators of public health information for both school staff and families. Already trusted as known medical professionals at school, nurses helped to untangle the confusing media messages around hygiene, masks, and contact tracing in support of their school community.

Migrant specialists became overnight bilingual tech supports by answering questions from anxious parents who struggled to find hotspots and other technology to work at home, often while speaking a language other than English. As parents and caregivers adjusted to the new role of "teacher-facilitators," support staff became their cheerleaders. One migrant specialist shared a photo that she received by text from a family who carefully wrapped rocks from their gravel road in paper to keep them clean and used them as manipulatives to help their young child to learn counting, addition, and subtraction. The homeless liaison shared how she advised families to continue learning even when lacking resources, and families responded. "I taught my grandson how to change the oil in my truck," said one grandfather. "We are reading recipes together and cooking," shared a mom and yet another said, "We are reading together every day from the Bible."

Lean into Change

Rarely does education have an opportunity to change as quickly as it changed during the spring of 2020. While the urgency of the pandemic closures created unmet needs and challenges, it also presented student support staff with opportunities to reimagine the work. The influential social and educational reformer John Dewey noted that we do not learn from experience, rather we learn from reflecting on experience (Dewey, 1933, p. 78). It's imperative that student services professionals pause long enough to "lean into" the positive changes that can emerge as best practices post-March 2020 school closing.

One example is to reconsider school-based mental health practices via telemedicine. Traditionally, students with mental health diagnoses in need of therapeutic counseling either missed school to attend therapy appointments or met with community mental health providers at school, often missing valuable seat-time in the process. During the COVID-19 school closures, community health providers quickly pivoted to use telemedicine to serve students. As schools reopen, student support staff should consider building telemedicine partnerships where students can engage in therapy via technology while at school. This model would also allow

Teachers, Leaders Care First for Students

for school psychologists, special education teachers, and others to engage with the mental health clinician and provide improved wraparound communication and support for students.

Other considerations as student support staff think about new ways of serving students:

- **Drop requirements for service provision that have been barriers in the past.** Many eligibility restrictions for access to services were lifted and loosened during COVID-19 closures. We found ourselves questioning if all provisions were necessary. Do families need to leave work to apply for benefits, or is there an easier way to do so virtually?

- **Build practices that have more differentiation than less.** For example, every form that is used by school psychologists, nurses, or social workers should have the option for an electronic signature. Meetings should allow parent participation by Zoom.

- **Reimagine parent engagement and involvement to build true partnerships** where family's own Funds of Knowledge (González et al., 2005) are valued as a true part of the educational experience. Funds of Knowledge are the abundant and unique social and intellectual resources that all households possess. These family strengths are sometimes invisible to educators who only see children at school; however, when families were forced into the role of teacher collaborator, parents drew upon their knowledge and skills to use to teach their children. For example, cooking was used to teach fractions and gardening to teach science. These valuable skills should be recognized, honored, and engaged when school reopens.

Time to Reimagine Student Support Services

Undoubtedly the disparate impact of remote learning and remote support illuminated the pre-existing inequities in our educational system. Student support staff now have an opportunity to re-vision student supports to reduce inequity. The challenge for all educators moving forward, including student support staff, will be to build new best practices that are more resistant to change and adversity. The COVID-19 pandemic is not the first and will not be the last disruption to education. Hurricane Katrina, September 11, 2001, and scores of other more localized and less documented crises have disrupted the education of our children. As we learn from the COVID-19 school closures, student support staff have the opportunity to be agile and innovative while learning to use new tools and gathering them into a new toolbox.

Dr. Meyers reminded us that the key to reimagining support services in schools was to rethink systems to ensure agility and responsiveness to a range of disruptive conditions. Addressing the unique social emotional needs of students in a virtual environment may be a difficult challenge for schools, likely more than developing online instructional materials. Advocates and pediatricians are seeing more trauma in children and anticipate the numbers will increase (Woodall, 2020) given the isolation created by COVID-19 (Elsen-Rooney, 2020).

Leading for Tomorrow

As teachers and leaders across the country responded to the unknowns of COVID-19, they were challenged to examine existing systems that were foundational to their work. As a result, new systems and responsibilities emerged as they:

- created new ways to meet the basic needs of children in a virtual environment;
- implemented new strategies to stay connected and provide students with needed social-emotional support;
- supported parents as they assumed new roles in educating their children at home through a virtual environment;
- struggled to ensure equitable learning opportunities given the vast array of home situations including access to technology and balancing parents work life with the support needed for virtual instruction;
- implemented new structures to meet the unique needs of students in customized programs such as students with Individualized Educational Plans or identified as an English Language Learner or Gifted.

Parents and their communities saw first-hand the heart and soul of educators and their timely and creative responses to support the many needs of their students while adopting new instructional models.

References

Bloch, E. (2020, May 5). "Mama is tired": After school closures, some families burn out on online classes, others thrive. *USA Today.* www.usatoday.com/story/news/education/2020/05/05/coronavirus-online-classes-school-closures-homeschool-burnout/3055101001/

Brenan, M. (2020, March 31). 42% of parents worry COVID-19 will affect child's education. *Gallup News.* https://news.gallup.com/poll/305819/parents-worry-covid-affect-child-education.aspx

Breunlin, E. (2020, April 13). How do you study online without a computer or Internet access? It's a reality for many Colorado kids. *The Colorado Sun.* https://coloradosun.com/2020/04/13/colorado-online-learning-remote-learning-students-teachers-coronavirus-Internet/

Child Abuse Prevention Treatment Act Reauthorization of 2010. (2010). P.L. 111–320, § 106(b)(2)(B)(ii).

Collopy, R. (2020, May 15). Educating students with disabilities during the time of COVID-19. *National Schoolchoice Week.* https://schoolchoiceweek.com/educating-students-with-disabilities-during-the-time-of-covid-19/

Coronavirus Aid, Relief, and Economic Security Act. (2020). S. 3548, 116th Cong., 2nd Sess. www.congress.gov/116/bills/hr748/BILLS-116hr748enr.pdf

Department of Education. (2020, March). Questions and answers on providing services to children with disabilities during the coronavirus disease 2019 outbreak. *ISBE.* www.isbe.net/Documents/qa-covid-19-03-12-2020.pdf

Dewey, J. (1933). *How we think.* D. C. Heath & Co.

Education Trust-New York. (2020, April 8). Poll: New York parents overwhelmingly concerned their children will fall behind academically during school closures. *Education Trust-New York*. https://newyork. edtrust.org/press-release/poll-new-york-parents-overwhelmingly-concerned-their-children-will-fall-behind-academically-during-school-closures/

Elsen-Rooney, M. (2020, April 20). NYC educators brace for student mental health challenges after coronavirus lockdown on classes ends. *New York Daily News*. www.nydailynews.com/coronavirus/ny-coronavirus-student-mental-health-issues-20200420-kgn3w7r6uzfx7nqijutuutwwiq-story.html

Fasso, G. I. (2020, April 6). Innovative schools find lessons—and opportunities—in remote learning. *EdSurge*. www.edsurge.com/news/2020-04-06-innovative-schools-find-lessons-and-opportunities-in-remote-learning

Gao, N., & Hill, L. (2020, April 10). Remote learning for English learners and special needs students during COVID-19. *Public Policy Institute of California*. www.ppic.org/blog/remote-learning-for-english-learners-and-special-needs-students-during-covid-19/

Gavin, J. (2020, March 31). Are special education services required in the time of COVID-19? *American Bar Association.* www.americanbar.org/groups/litigation/committees/childrens-rights/articles/2020/are-special-education-services-required-in-the-time-of-covid19/

Gilreath, A. (2020, May 6). Without in-person classes, many students have essentially gone missing, teachers say. *USA Today*. www.usatoday.com/story/news/education/2020/05/04/coronavirus-thousands-students-sc-not-doing-their-school-work/3078809001/

González, N., Moll, L., & Amanti, C. (2005). *Funds of knowledge: Theorizing practices in households, communities, and classrooms*. Routledge.

Jacobson, L. (2020, April 13). Ed, tech coalition launches resource for remotely serving special needs students. *Education Dive.* www.educationdive.com/news/ed-tech-coalition-launches-resource-for-remotely-serving-special-needs-stu/575747/

Jarrett, L., & Pomrenze, Y. (2020, May 4). Experts caution "covid slide" looming for children out of school. *CNN US*. www.cnn.com/2020/05/04/us/coronavirus-education-online-school-slide-wellness/index.html

Kamenetz, A. (2020, April 28). Child sexual abuse reports are on the rise amid lockdown orders. *NPR*. www.npr.org/sections/coronavirus-live-updates/2020/04/28/847251985/child-sexual-abuse-reports-are-on-the-rise-amid-lockdown-orders

Kuhfeld, M., & Tarasawa, B. (2020, April). The COVID-19 slide: What summer learning loss can tell us about the potential impact of school closures on student academic achievement. *NWEA Research*. www.nwea.org/content/uploads/2020/05/Collaborative-Brief_Covid19-Slide-APR20.pdf

Maslow, A. H. (1943). A theory of human motivation. *Psychological Review, 50*(4), 370–396. https://doi.org/10.1037/h0054346

McLeod, S. (2020, March 20). Maslow's hierarchy of needs. *SimplyPsychology*. www.simplypsychology.org/maslow.html

Modan, N. (2020, April 3). Would IDEA waivers benefit districts during school closures? *Education Dive*. www.educationdive.com/news/would-idea-waivers-benefit-districts-during-school-closures/575408/

Mundy, K., & Hares, S. (2020, April 16). Equity-focused approaches to learning loss during COVID-19. *Center for Global Development*. www.cgdev.org/blog/equity-focused-approaches-learning-loss-during-covid-19

Rothstein, R. (2020, April 13). The coronavirus will explode achievement gaps in education. *Shelterforce*. https://shelterforce.org/2020/04/13/the-coronavirus-will-explode-achievement-gaps-in-education/

Strauss, V. (2020, April 17). Why COVID-19 will "explode" existing academic achievement gaps. *The Washington Post*. www.washingtonpost.com/education/2020/04/17/why-covid-19-will-explode-existing-academic-achievement-gaps/

USAFacts. (2020, April 7). More than 9 million children lack internet access at home for online learning. *USAFacts*. https://usafacts.org/articles/internet-access-students-at-home/

Walker, T. (2020, April 15). Social-emotional learning should be priority during COVID-19 crisis. *NEA Today*. http://neatoday.org/2020/04/15/social-emotional-learning-during-covid/?mkt_tok=eyJpIjoiWkdZMIlq Vm1NVEE1WkRWbSIsInQiOiJ5TjJucGVkTVVWVkFZVmV0ZVpKTHl 0ZFR0b0lLVVlDVHdnTVoxazlqRWNQMytBQ21NS0txQlYrZUxva3h ZYmJ0YjNUQ0kyZXhUbzBQWlBwUG44a0crV1wvd0ZHS0hKM21l bGl1XC9zMWlZZjh4bVVRSVwvVnZ5TlpvdHdsdjJYbVwvb1YifQ%3 D%3D

Woodall, C. (2020, May 13). As hospitals see more severe child abuse injuries during coronavirus, "the worst is yet to come." *USA Today*. www.usatoday.com/story/news/nation/2020/05/13/hospitals-seeing-more-severe-child-abuse-injuries-during-coronavirus/3116395001/

Zerotothree. (2020, April 14). Young children at home during the COVID-19 outbreak: The importance of self-care. *Zerotothree*. www.zerotothree. org/resources/3262-young-children-at-home-during-the-covid-19-outbreak-the-importance-of-self-care

Short-term Response, Long-term Implications

In This Chapter...	
Introduction	50
Responding to Students' Basic Needs	51
Narrative: *Agility and Adaptability: Two Keys to Future*	
Success	53
Creating New Systems	56
Narrative: *The COVID-19 Impact on School Design*	60
The New Normal	64
Narrative: *Disruption Accelerates Transformation and*	
Strengthens Community	67
Leading for Tomorrow	72
References	73

Introduction

The old saying that "schools have not changed dramatically over the last century" does hold merit, some of the time. Historically, schools have gone through shifts in instructional approaches such as personalized learning; however, the tension to snap back to traditional approaches and practices remains. In many ways, educational change is like a rubber band. It can be stretched to take on a new shape by wrapping it around something new, but the tension remains to snap back to its original shape.

The ability to enact change in response to COVID-19 and the fast-paced nature of new information becoming available daily set a new course for schools and districts. Leaders and teachers remain in a state of flux as they develop short-term responses that impact existing systems. There was no playbook to consult; yet, for just about every decision, there would be a long-term impact. In this chapter, responding to students' basic needs, creating new approaches, and the new normal are examined.

Responding to Students' Basic Needs

The primary focus for schools was on the physical and social emotional safety of staff and students. Superintendents and their districts, school, and community teams were entering unfamiliar territory. Risk and turbulence required leaders to rethink every system to navigate this pandemic. With unknown and quickly changing landscapes, creating confidence was critical and required making timely decisions, providing essential information, and using multiple communication streams with continuous feedback loops.

Shifting Landscapes

The first priority was to meet children's basic needs of food and safety while simultaneously ramping-up an instructional program embedded in a virtual environment. Within a day or two of closing schools, systems began providing breakfast and lunches to millions of students across the country. Through the courageous efforts of food service staff members and bus drivers, buses stocked with meals were seen in school and mall parking lots, community centers, and in other accessible locations.

Teachers and school personnel understood the urgency to connect with students to ensure their well-being. Teachers sought ways to stay connected given the isolation from their peers (Blackburn, 2020). Social media highlighted schools, systems, and teachers reaching out to their

Short-term Response, Long-term Implications

students in ways such as holding neighborhood parades for the students enrolled in their schools, making signs to place in their yards, and holding virtual graduation ceremonies.

Tomorrow Became Today

Access to resources varied greatly across school districts. While some districts already engaged in online scheduled facetime, others had access only to "canned" materials and programs used to remediate or to supplement direct instruction. Systems without technology relied on paper and pencil units picked up and returned to school. For some school leaders and teachers, moving into a virtual environment was planned but to be implemented in a gradual process. However, the COVID-19 response required an almost instant response. The good news is that the resistance to the use of technology as the primary means of instruction disappeared immediately as teachers saw this change as the only option available to teach their students (Ascione, 2020). The new challenge became the lack of continuity and consistency in students' experiences within schools and across districts and states.

The many unknowns about COVID-19 made planning at all levels of the school district difficult and short-term at best. For most, it was like walking in the dark with only a short stick to help navigate what was ahead. Everyday yielded new, often tentative information that changed what tomorrow would bring. School leaders struggled to make decisions today for what was unknown about tomorrow.

The shifting landscape required agility, adaptability, and grace as described by Dr. Donald E. Robertson, Jr. the Chief Schools Officer in the Virginia Beach City Public Schools (VBCPS) located in Virginia Beach, Virginia. VBCPS is an urban system that serves 66,820 students supported by 15,027 teachers, staff, and administrators. Dr. Robertson, Jr. has served for 32 years in VBCPS as a teacher and coach, assistant principal, principal, assistant superintendent, and chief strategy and innovation officer.

In this Narrative, Dr. Robertson, Jr. shared insights about the agility and adaptability that school systems need as they focused on moving forward to be ready for future adaptation whether it was due to a pandemic or another disruptive force.

Dr. Donald E. Robertson, Jr.
Chief Strategy and Innovation Officer
Virginia Beach City Public Schools
Virginia Beach, VA

Agility and Adaptability: Two Keys to Future Success

Who would have predicted at the end of 2019, or at any other time in the last century, that in 2020 the world would be essentially shut down by a pandemic? The answer is no one. In March of 2020, school divisions across the United States were suddenly closed, causing millions of students to be removed from the school setting well before the end of the school year, and educators to be tasked with continuing education in a setting that didn't include that which was most familiar, in-person and inside a school building.

For Virginia Beach City Public Schools, without knowing it, we had been establishing practices over the past ten years that have made this transition somewhat manageable. In hindsight this work that began in 2010 promoted our ability to be *adaptable* and *agile* in the face of this sudden change. In the area of infrastructure and resources, the work of the past ten years helped us to be able to quickly transition to a fully online virtual learning environment. These efforts included:

- Ten years ago, we partnered with the city to significantly expand our broadband services to all areas of the city, which gave us the ability to have the needed fiber network and Wi-Fi services to reach all students and families.

- Five years ago, we began moving to 1:1 for all students and we reached that plateau in 2019–2020. In addition, five years ago we began researching a learning management system that would house our curriculum, assessments, and link to all of our online resources.

- Three years ago, we chose the learning management system Schoology and strategically rolled out the platform to schools. This year, all schools were fully implementing Schoology to support teaching and learning.

Short-term Response, Long-term Implications

- Finally, two years ago we embedded two virtual learning days into our school calendar and asked our teachers to deliver virtual learning experiences to all K-12 students.

Despite the existence of these resources, I would not say our staff were prepared to be suddenly thrust into a full virtual environment. According to a recent division technology survey, a slight majority of staff indicated they were prepared to deliver a lesson in an online environment. Approximately 20% of survey respondents indicated they needed substantial additional professional development to be able to deliver learning in an online environment. As a result, we developed a series of learning plans (Continuity to Emergency) for all students and provided staff with one day per week to receive professional development (PD) of their choosing to support teaching and learning in an online environment. These PD sessions were provided by central office specialists and by school-based teacher leaders. The other four days per week were designed to provide teachers with asynchronous learning experiences to deliver to their students and designated office hours to provide synchronous support to their students.

Recognizing our students would need as much structure as possible we designed a learning plan that was based in flexibility and focused on only the most essential learning standards/objectives. Students were expected to participate by accessing the content via Schoology, interacting with the teacher as needed, and by submitting work for one learning experience per week per course. If students had Wi-Fi or device issues, they were directed to call their school or the division help center where support was provided up to and including device repair, delivery of hotspots, and troubleshooting.

We were fortunate that all students had been provided with four virtual learning days over the past two years to experience remote, asynchronous learning. Our last virtual learning day occurred on March 5, 2020, just one week prior to the close of our schools.

The biggest impact of this sudden closure was with our students with disabilities (SWD), Title I, Section 504, and English Language Learners (ELL). Each group demonstrated a significant need for personal interaction with a teacher which cannot be replicated under any online system. To help address this challenge, all students with disabilities had a virtual IEP meeting with staff to add distance learning and accommodations to their

IEPs. For the other student groups that often struggle (ELL, Section 504, Free and Reduced Lunch), teachers provided small-group virtual experiences to support learning.

This experience has forever changed the face of instruction in VBCPS. When we eventually return to school, the use of technology to meet staff, student and family needs will become commonplace. Teachers will regularly embed enrichment and remediation online resources into their daily learning plans; move beyond traditional assessments to include allowing students to submit demonstrations of learning, artifacts, and portfolios; recognize it is no longer as important to show *what you know* but to show *what you can do with what you know*. Students will better leverage technology to meet their learning needs and to demonstrate what they know and are able to do. Finally, parents will be better prepared to access resources to support their child's learning needs, real-time school performance data, and become a partner in their child's learning.

Insights to Lead During the Next Storm

It is often stated that "within every dark cloud is a silver lining." Based on this experience, I have developed new insights that will help prepare me and the system for the next storm. These include:

- Take time to develop communication around the "why." In a crisis, people need to understand why a change is necessary. Using data to support the need yields better results.
- Seek staff and community thoughts on what they view as the challenges ahead. This is not input in decision-making but can inform decision-making.
- Build staff capacity to understand and use the "why" to create the "what" and implement the "how" in their own setting.
- Professional development is critical for success and must be needs-based, ongoing, and collaborative.
- Seek to expand your network of thought partners. Sharing ideas, problems and solutions will not only yield far better results but also affirm your work.
- Embrace transformation and the need to pivot as circumstances warrant.

- Embrace the "sprint cycle" of completing complex tasks. This process lends itself well to keeping people focused and engaged in a task that is designed to be accomplished in a 2–4-week timeframe.

- Find *your* work–life balance, as resilience and adaptability are key to your mental health and the success of your home and work needs/plans.

In closing, I hope this testimony helps you and your team navigate these uncharted waters. Your leadership matters in everything you say, you do, and don't do. Listen more, speak less, and recognize this is an adaptive challenge and will require everyone to think and act differently at one time or another. Good luck and know I am in this fight with you!

Dr. Robertson, Jr. articulated the challenges for Virginia Beach brought forth with COVID-19 even though they were already shifting instructional delivery systems. Nonetheless, instituting this level of change required everyone to think and act differently.

Creating New Systems

In moving forward in planning for an unknown future, all systems (e.g., instruction, transportation, health services, etc.) require review to ensure a safe environment. New systems must become the norm across areas including instruction, technology, transportation, custodial, health, and building design and facilities.

Systems

Instruction. Moving the classroom to a fully virtual space changed the role of the teacher because they were now physically distanced from students. This shift, although different than in person, can support a learner-centric approach in a virtual environment as elaborated in Table 3.1.

Short-term Response, Long-term Implications

Table 3.1 Learner-centric approaches and questions in a virtual environment

Learner-centric in a virtual environment	*Questions to transform instruction post-COVID-19 in a virtual environment*
All components are designed for the education experience to be adaptable to the needs and potential of each learner and supports the highest possible outcomes for each and every learner (Education Reimagined, 2015, p. 5).	1. How are units designed and student work evaluated? 2. How do you engage students and provide feedback? 3. How do you differentiate instruction to meet varied learning styles? 4. Will learning be linear by grades or competency based? 5. How do you create personal contacts and build relationships with students?

Moving to a virtual environment is not about replicating existing classroom instructional designs with a teacher in the classroom. The approach is no longer about "in" school versus "out of" school—it is about new thinking on how to challenge individual learners at anytime from anywhere. Chapter 4, "Teaching as We Knew It," examines more fully teaching and learning.

Technology. The foundation for school transformation to virtual design first requires a robust technology infrastructure. In the flurry for school districts to put devices in every student's hands, attention needed to include Internet access which continues to be the largest obstacle when schools look to include all students. However, creating access is more than placing devices in students' hands. It requires school infrastructures including support for beginning users and parents, a robust digital curriculum, systems for device acquisitions and repairs, security software, and the bandwidth to handle the increase in users.

Transportation. School transportation services, getting students to and from school, is probably the most overlooked system in education yet influences many school functions from start and stop times, field trips, and extracurricular activities. In the United States in 2019, 25 million children stepped on 475,000 school buses and were dropped off at the schoolhouse doors every morning (NRT Bus Inc., n.d.). Transportation leaders are fielding the same kind of tough questions as school and district leaders as COVID-19 changes much of how they operate. Social distancing protocols, cleaning protocols, and other systems need to be reexamined and when schools open, transportation leaders will be required to rethink their overall approach to transporting students. Table 3.2 examines areas that need to be considered by school transportation divisions.

Custodial. As schools prepare to open, no one is more on the front-lines than school custodians. School facilities cannot open unless custodial operations are in place to keep the school environment safe. With COVID-19, the critical role of building custodians is finally being recognized by the public.

Building cleanliness and safety protocols today have very different standards as compared to those pre-COVID-19. The post-COVID-19

Table 3.2 School transportation system considerations

Impacted area	Considerations
Bus routes	1. The bus capacity limits with social distancing. 2. Need for additional busses. 3. Number of parents selecting virtual instructional delivery vs in school. 4. School schedule and start and stop times.
Bus drivers	1. Availability – larger number of drivers were laid off and assumed other jobs, while other areas experienced bus driver shortages. 2. Health – some bus drivers are retired and are at greater health risk. 3. Time for training and certifying new drivers. 4. Overall less interest in being a bus driver. 5. Protective wear such as masks.
Student safety	1. Requires additional personnel on a bus other than the bus driver. 2. Monitoring social distancing. 3. Bus stop and drop offs. 4. Curricular and extracurricular activities. 5. Bus retrofits. 6. Protective wear such as masks.
Cleaning	1. New cleaning protocols and schedule. 2. Cleaning and disinfecting equipment. 3. Added personnel. 4. Time – when do you clean buses?

cleaning and disinfecting protocols outlined by the Centers for Disease Control and Prevention (CDC, 2020) changed the responsibilities of custodians and are more comprehensive:

- Cleaning refers to the removal of germs, dirt, and impurities from surfaces. It does not kill germs, but by removing them, it lowers their numbers and the risk of spreading infection.
- Disinfecting refers to using chemicals, for example, EPA-registered disinfectants, to kill germs on surfaces. This process does not necessarily clean dirty surfaces or remove germs, but by killing germs on a surface *after* cleaning, it can further lower the risk of spreading infection (CDC, 2020, para. 6–7).

A detailed yet flexible plan as illustrated in Table 3.3 will require a very different plan than previously used in schools.

Table 3.3 School custodial considerations

Planning	Considerations
Staff safety	1. Wear personal protective equipment (PPE). 2. Safe use of products—read labels. 3. Safe storage of products. 4. Routinely test for COVID-19.
Evaluate	1. Which surfaces need cleaning and/or disinfecting? 2. Surface types? 3. Frequency in which surfaces are touched? 4. Toxicity of products used?
Implement	1. Create needed staffing schedules. 2. Document and train on new protocols. 3. Focus on safety. 4. Communication to students, staff, and parents.
Monitor and adjust	1. Keep up to date on COVID-19 changes, effective protocols, and products. 2. Remain flexible. 3. Collect feedback and recommendations for improvements.

Adapted from CDC (2020). Note: These considerations may change as more information on COVID-19 becomes available.

Facility Design. Schools have made many substantive changes to not only cleaning their facilities, but also in making modifications to support procedures aligned to new safety measures. Schools will need to commit substantial resources to retrofit buildings to accommodate social distancing efforts, reduce hallway bottlenecks, provide hand-sanitizing stations, secure protective shields, and rethink the use of common spaces such as cafeterias and gymnasiums.

With a background in instructional leadership, former school superintendent, Dr. Douglas Huntley, teamed up with the architect group CSArch to explore the impact of COVID-19 on the future of school design. Dr. Huntley served as the superintendent of the Queensbury Union Free School District, located in Queensbury, New York, with an enrollment of 3,200 students K-12. As the Senior Associate at CSArch, Dr. Huntley, shared his thoughts on the changes needed in school design to address the health and safety of students as well as the technology demands as schools returned to school post-COVID-19.

Douglas Huntley, Ed.D.
Senior Associate, CSArch
Albany, NY

The COVID-19 Impact on School Design

Years from now when we look back on the impact of COVID-19 on schools, we predict a number of physical modifications to the built environment which will pale only in comparison to the major changes in education in the coming months and years. While building designs and instructional models will change, we do not expect to change the way schools and their learning environments provide a sense of stability, connectedness, spirit-lifting, and daily focus.

Physical Facilities Changes Needed in the Present

Already trending, we should see a continued increase in the demand for automation, with schools considering touchless lighting and temperature controls, motion-activated doors, and voice-activated elevators. The use of hands-free dispensers for face masks and synthetic gloves and touchless hand washing and sanitizing stations may become commonplace. And security vestibules could be equipped with fever-detecting features to measure body temperature.

Bathrooms will likely receive the greatest focus, with even more touch-free devices. The controversial topic of *bathrooms without doors* may gain more traction, with a code-permitting solution required that will balance the need for privacy and focus on student health.

From shared computers, desks, tables, doors, vending machines, and bathroom facilities, communal surfaces are widespread in school buildings, and all are potential sources of contagion. In addition to choosing easy-to-clean, non-porous materials, we can expect to see a greater use of materials with antimicrobial properties in building construction and in the selection of interior fabrics and finishes.

Full-time robotics can help as well. For example, robotic floor cleaners can operate around the clock constantly keeping floors clean and sanitary, allowing cleaners and custodians to focus on other high-priority issues. Small storage areas with recharging capabilities will need to be considered in future school design or redesign.

The strategic design and installation of modern HVAC systems is another critical factor in the prevention of disease and germ spreading, as modern equipment can circulate and change air quickly, thus cleansing the air frequently and regularly. Used by many hospitals and health care facilities to minimize the transmission of airborne pathogens, the addition of UVC airstream disinfection is an engineering design solution schools may consider, although it could come at a high cost for equipment, operation, and maintenance. If properly sized and installed, UVC airstream disinfection can inactivate microorganisms like bacteria, fungi, and viruses.

Research has also suggested a link between indoor relative humidity (ranging from 40 to 60%) and reduced contagion. While humidity levels must be taken into consideration with the impact of condensation on building materials, this link could have implications on the future design of building envelopes.

Closing the Digital Divide

For districts with widespread connectivity and 1:1 technology already embedded in daily learning, education continues. Unfortunately, for districts without universally available digital access, the continuation of

Short-term Response, Long-term Implications

teaching and learning takes a different route. Here the digital divide is clearly evident and only increases as time goes on, creating serious inequities in education.

When we think about the future of school design, perhaps the highest priority is a strongly embedded technology platform for teaching, learning, safety, and business functions. Implemented in tandem with a robust technology plan and as an essential element of a capital improvement project, a school's network in a post-coronavirus world will require stronger, more efficient, and more stable infrastructure to meet the needs of students and the community.

Improving Social Distancing

The need for social distancing has us rethinking the way common areas in public schools are designed. With the continued goal to allow students and community members to assemble, school design may refocus to encourage spreading out, with greater separation in places like gymnasiums, cafeterias, auditoriums, corridors, and classrooms. In the immediate future, classrooms will benefit from flexible furniture to configure desks further apart and facing the same direction, thereby reducing the typical class size and the transmission of germs.

Social distancing will naturally encourage small group breakouts, an upward trend we've been seeing in schools for several years. This has led to the design of alternative learning environments such as smaller breakout rooms and extended learning areas for students. Providing enrichment opportunities, these spaces are based outside of the traditional classroom and promote small groups and personalized instruction.

Planning for the Future

Like the response to the Ice Storm of 1998, Hurricane Katrina, and 9/11, our public-school system has once again proven its resilience in the wake of COVID-19. Each of these catastrophes created the need for our schools to respond and adapt into newer models, increasing and expanding their roles and assuming greater responsibilities.

As schools engage in building projects in the future, they may wish to design their facilities to be more adaptable. For instance, certain school buildings like a field house or gymnasium could be designed to be easily converted into temporary space for emergency shelters or hospitals. High schools are "good conversion options because they are found in almost all communities, are big enough to house 200 to 500 COVID-19 patients..., have wide corridors, and have mostly nonporous durable surfaces for easy cleaning" (Caulfield, 2020).

Final Thoughts

Needed for now and the foreseeable future are safe and healthy school environments that are flexible enough to accommodate new instructional designs. These types of designs are needed given that emerging forces are not always known, such as in the current pandemic. To imagine school structures to support virtual schooling requires new thinking about facility designs. Designing for the unknown requires leaders to be open to new approaches in designing school facilities.

Dr. Huntley highlighted the importance of school facility design to create environments that support new instructional designs. His recommendations provided critical perspectives as leaders developed new systems for providing health services and emerging instructional models.

Health Services. Health service programs range from systems that are reactive to day-to-day issues and provide services mostly centered around student medications, often with the use of part-time and traveling nurses or their equivalent. Some systems have full service health clinics in their schools to support students and their families. With COVID-19, every system will need to be evaluated, modified, or completely redesigned to fulfill new and emerging health requirements.

Similar to immediately providing meals to students, schools needed to support the medical needs of students by first reaching out to medically fragile students. Anderson and Caseman (2020) recommend that schools should:

- Coordinate with health center providers and administrators to ensure that children with physical and mental health needs can access appropriate services.
- Communicate with parents and students about how to access health care services, particularly in isolated areas that lack an accessible clinic.

Short-term Response, Long-term Implications

- Consider permitting school-based health centers to remain open if schools themselves are minimally staffed.
- Allow school-based health centers to pivot to a telehealth model and communicate the new protocols and procedures with students and staff.
- Because of HIPAA regulations, health center staff will need to reach out to students and families who use the center regarding alternative health care options.

(Anderson & Caseman, 2020, para. 6–10)

As school leaders prepare for students to return, school nurses and health care employees provide critical information required in the decision-making processes to ensure health practices are in place.

Throughout COVID-19, the National Association of School Nurses (2020) steadily updated their guidance on how to leverage the expertise of professionals in the field. A sample school opening framework is outlined in Table 3.4.

With information and guidance continually being updated, school leaders will need to remain flexible and nimble, but not unstable. The challenges of COVID-19 will provide valuable insight into the systems of yesterday and how their designs will evolve as the new normal.

The New Normal

The known as schools move forward is the unknown. The need to implement safety procedures and protocols, and the implementation of virtual environments has intensified the efforts to create and leverage new systems. School leaders are well aware of how changes made today in response to COVID-19 may remain as either fully intact or in some modified form as they move ahead in an unknown space.

Sustainability

While there are no predictions at this time of what systems will remain intact, school leaders will need to think through how decisions are made for programs to be sustained or not. Sustainability can be viewed through multiple

Short-term Response, Long-term Implications

Table 3.4 School health considerations

Contribution	Expertise
Leadership	1. Connect to local and state experts. 2. Evaluate the ability and use of resources. 3. Recommend policies and procedures for students and staff excluded for presumed or diagnosed with COVID-19. 4. Advocate for students, staff, and parents to local, state, and national organizations, and policy makers.
Quality improvement	1. Collect critical data to support individuals and guide system-level decisions. 2. Share data and collaborate.
Care coordination	1. Coordinate with student families and health teams. 2. Provide trauma-informed practices. 3. Provide recommendations on unmet needs of medically fragile students. 4. Recommend protocols for students who have symptoms of COVID-19.
Public health	1. Provide expertise in culturally competent health practices. 2. Provide guidance on school safety procedures. 3. Support community agencies and use as a source of information.

lenses. From one perspective, sustainability identifies a set of factors and conditions for a specific intervention. Another perspective views sustainability from an ecological or complex system view. This perspective acknowledges the interconnections between contextual and environmental conditions in connection to the intervention (Stirman et al., 2012). Both perspectives are important to sustain changes in the traditional constructs that no longer produce the desired results in the short and long term.

In education, developing and sustaining new systems creates a tension to return to how systems were before. In the business environment, where innovation is the foundation for success, creating a collective sense of purpose and action relies on the expertise of those in the organization. For school leaders moving forward, using an innovation framework for organizational sustainability is important as decisions are made about what the new normal will look like in their schools and districts.

Leadership for Sustainability

Evaluating and sustaining innovations starts at the top of the organization where leaders see the need for change and creativity. In the COVID-19 pandemic, many new innovations in systems have emerged from the safety requirements and in the transitions to a virtual environment. Based on Adler and Karlsberg's (2005) work, sustaining innovations—similar to what has been experienced during COVID-19—requires the right organizational conditions that include:

- **Clear direction:** Understanding that change and innovation is important to improve results.
- **Open communication:** Creating multiple communication streams that connect at every level of the organization and build trusting exchanges of ideas.
- **Reduced bureaucracy:** New ideas are welcome and can be implemented in a timely manner without continuous roadblocks and resistance.
- **Ownership:** Providing employees with commentary on their value to the organizations is a powerful incentive.
- **Recognition and incentives:** Providing recognition and incentives to the whole rather than individuals in supporting an innovative culture.
- **Risk and failure:** Understanding that not everything will create the desired results—which is healthy.
- **Elimination:** If innovations do not work, discontinue, and move on to other solutions.

Sustaining change to improve student achievement, whether in a COVID-19 pandemic or not, is not an easy endeavor for educational leaders especially when entering the unknown.

Today, educational leaders can no longer rely on the systems of the past in seeking solutions as the conditions related to COVID-19 are constantly changing. However, in creating the new normal, educational leaders must understand the dynamics of change and sustainability as they leverage what is known using the expertise of teachers, parents, and members of the community

Using reflective questioning to move his system forward, Dr. Brian Troop, superintendent of the suburban Ephrata Area School District (EASD) located in Ephrata, Pennsylvania, shared insights about this process. EASD serves 4,290 K-12 students supported by 312 classroom teachers and 256 support staff. In 2018, EASD received a letter of recognition from the Pennsylvania Department of Education for its Life-Ready Graduate work, and the system was selected as a host sight for the AASA Digital Consortium (now called the Transformational Leadership Consortium) in March of 2019.

Dr. Troop's initial response to COVID-19 was first to understand and support the immediate needs of teachers and families through transparent two-way communication and stressing the expectations of existing school processes. In his Narrative, Dr. Troop was confident that the return to a new normal was likely to be much different than the one pre-COVID-19.

Brian Troop, Ed.D.
Superintendent
Ephrata Area School District
Ephrata, PA

Disruption Accelerates Transformation and Strengthens Community

The Ephrata Area School District (EASD) serves approximately 4,200 students and is located about an hour west of Philadelphia. Our community is mostly blue-collar, filled with hard-working and proud citizens who want the best for their children and who are supportive of our District mission, which reads in part:

> to provide all students a secure learning environment and exemplary academic programs that inspire all students to *reach their full potential.*

Over the past five years, the District administration has engaged the Board, staff, parents, business leaders, alumni, and the community at large in a reflective process aimed at answering the general question "What is the purpose of public education in the 21st century?" and three more specific questions of (a) What knowledge, skills, and dispositions do graduates need to *reach their full potential* in life?, (b) What do we know about how to engage students toward the development of these traits?, and (c) What type of educational program(s) do we have the capacity to deliver?

While these may be some of the same questions asked in the late 1800s when public education was standardized to resemble the factory model we live with today, our collective efforts helped us to identify areas where we believed we could do better, given the 21st-century context in which we exist. This transformational work has led to several notable accomplishments, including:

- a set of beliefs that emphasizes trusting relationships and the importance of skills and dispositions beyond what can be easily tested and prioritizes the use of technology in our response to a rapidly changing world;

- a community-endorsed portrait of a graduate, called the Ephrata Life Ready Graduate (LRG), that serves as a north star toward which all District programs can be aligned;

- a District-wide instructional model built around a student-centered environment that guides unit and lesson design in kindergarten through twelfth grade;

- a K-12 continuum of multidisciplinary cornerstone projects that integrates course competencies and learning targets with LRG traits, all delivered through the use of outside experts and community connections.

As evidenced by this list of structural improvements and innovations, the EASD community had been on a path marked by what we thought was rapid change and realignment to a 21st-century vision. On March 13, 2020, however, an entirely new rate of change was thrust upon us all and demanded immediate attention.

Transparent Communication

At EASD, our initial response to the sudden closure of schools had two primary components. The first was to understand and support the immediate needs of teachers and families through transparent two-way communication. This dialogue guided us in establishing clear expectations on specific parts of the educational process, such as attendance, grading, etc., as well as addressing the technology and access issues that existed on both sides of the student–teacher relationship.

The second component was to elevate the quality of work by staff—and consequently students—through professional learning, contextualizing the instructional model and prioritization of the curriculum for the remainder of the school year. We understood that this emergency online instruction needed to be accessible to all and prioritized so we could ensure students had the opportunity to be prepared for the next step on their learning path, even though we knew the online instructional mode was not the best match for every student or curricular unit.

Professional Learning Offers Support

Sadly, there were cases when the switch to online presented enough of an obstacle to derail progress by students and staff toward learning goals. Collectively, we realized that not all instructional activities and lesson/unit plans can simply be "plugged-in" and delivered online. Hence the focus on our professional learning sessions offered support to teachers in the adaptation of our instructional design to be effective in the virtual instruction world. The good news was that teachers who were more advanced in their use of instructional technology and who had invested more attention into competency-based curricular work transitioned to the online modality more easily. These insights have proven valuable and helped inform school reopening work and ongoing professional learning.

Looking Ahead

Looking ahead, we are not planning on our education system returning to exactly what it looked like in the pre-pandemic era. Our current menu of instructional delivery modes enables students to "switch lanes" from our in-person Modified Traditional mode to our at-home Online Learning mode at a moment's notice. Teachers plan each day for a group of students to be engaged

Short-term Response, Long-term Implications

from the classroom alongside those joining via technology from home. As members of the same virtual classroom, logging in from the location of their choosing, all students participate in the same instruction, collaborative dialogue, and application activities designed for this environment—thus bridging the gap between those at school and those who need to stay home for family or health reasons. While some families have elected for their child to receive all of their instruction in the physical classroom, others have opted for two days at school and three at home each week.

Allowing choice for parents and flexibility within our instructional framework have both paid dividends in our ability to partner with and support families as they respond to how the pandemic has individually disrupted their lives. Offering multiple options and the ability for students to switch lanes will continue to be priorities of the EASD instructional program.

There can be no dispute that the world is rapidly changing. The vast and continuing impact of the COVID-19 pandemic will continue to reshape society and transform many aspects of our school communities. As the local public-school district, we are charged to be responsive to society's shifting immediate and long-term needs. By maintaining a focus on the broad and specific purpose of public education, engaging in transparent communication about the challenges we will face, and responding with empathy, unity, and resilience, public education can continue to inspire graduates, and their communities, to reach their full potential.

Dr. Troop understood the impact of COVID-19 on the district's direction of redefining the classroom. While the current pandemic has changed their trajectory in creating new instructional designs, teachers embraced new opportunities to offer flexible choices and to further define priorities for the future. The high level of involvement was due, in part, to engaging internal stakeholders in the process to understand and respect the value of their expertise.

Engaging from the Inside

Leaders play a critical role in how they advance change by engaging stakeholders in processes that allow for the voices from the field to be involved in making decisions and developing plans. This type of involvement for teachers must be central to moving forward in further defining the next steps for this new reality. Teachers are highly motivated and ready to make change when their expertise is valued, their opinions matter, and they work in an environment where they are empowered to do their best work. Oftentimes the expected outcomes teachers and leaders seek appear different, but in reality, it is much more about the process and their work environment.

Teachers learned a great deal from the experiences of moving the instructional life of the classroom to a virtual environment. They provide invaluable insights into what worked, what did not work so well, and what could possibly work. According to Kutylo (2019) "Educators want change that values their voice, their context, and their motivations" (para. 6). As schools made enormous changes in response to COVID-19, leaders must understand the change process through the lens of teachers as systems create the new normal. Kutylo further identifies what teachers see as important as they adopt new practices that:

1. *Help me lead the way in improving my school.* Teachers are eager to demonstrate their value as contributors to broader school improvement.
2. *Help me find manageable ways to engage and challenge more of my students in a way that's manageable.* Teachers are open to new strategies that they feel will help them engage students they have struggled to reach, but must feel these strategies are practical to incorporate into their existing practices and routines.
3. *Help me replace a broken instructional model so I can reach each student.* Teachers struggle constantly with a sense that they aren't living up to their responsibilities to their students. These teachers seek approaches that will help them completely transform their approach to instruction.
4. *Help me to not fall behind on my school's new initiative.* Teachers are not actively looking for new solutions. New practices—like integrating technology—seem like an added layer of complexity on top of already demanding work. They are not convinced that a new practice will be better than strategies they have developed through years of experience. However, as the solution scales within their district, they feel they have no choice but to adopt it.

(Kutylo, 2019, para. 10–13, emphasis in the original)

Short-term Response, Long-term Implications

Leading the change process is a balancing act but is easier to navigate and sustain by understanding the dynamics of schools and the will of teachers. Change is best sustained from the inside-out rather than the outside-in.

While the tension to return to the "old" normal exists and much focus is on what is going to happen today, school leaders must also be thinking beyond the COVID-19 logistics. Urgency to change during this pandemic has created new opportunities for school leaders and teachers to sustain more effective system changes to address the longstanding issues of performance and inequities. What will be the "new" normal? Time will tell.

Leading for Tomorrow

The "normal" of schooling across the country changed within days, even hours, as schools shut their doors and moved to a virtual environment in response to COVID-19. For schools to open in the short term and to sustain themselves over the long term, they need to examine how to function differently by:

- establishing a level of educational continuity amid an environment of rapid change;
- examining current systems such as instructional delivery, technology, transportation, custodial, and health to determine what safety changes would be required when schools reopened;
- evaluating and addressing existing learning gaps and those created when schools moved quickly to a fully virtual environment;
- ensuring successful innovations are sustained given a propensity for new programs to "snap back" to what existed pre-COVID-19;
- engaging teachers by tapping into their knowledge base and experiences as leaders make decisions on how to move forward.

Teachers and leaders made monumental changes in systems such as custodial, transportation, technology and medical support required to reopen their schools for a return to in-person instruction.

References

Adler, J., & Karlsberg, R. (2005, June 9). 7 strategies for sustained innovation. *Innovation Management.* https://innovationmanagement.se/imtool-articles/7-strategies-for-sustained-innovation/

Anderson, S., & Caseman, K. (2020, March 18). School-based health centers can deliver care to vulnerable populations during the COVID-19 pandemic. *Child Trends.* www.childtrends.org/school-based-health-centers-can-deliver-care-to-vulnerable-populations-during-the-covid-19-pandemic

Ascione, L. (2020, April 23). How this district moved online with a moment's notice. *eSchool News.* www.eschoolnews.com/2020/04/23/how-this-district-moved-online-with-a-moments-notice/?all

Blackburn, S. (2020, April 28). Why districts need to provide mental health services during COVID-19, report reveals. *District Administration.* https://districtadministration.com/districts-provide-school-mental-health-services-school-health-counseling-covid-19?oly_enc_id=6799J8347367J8A

Caulfield, J. (2020, April 7). How to turn a high school into a patient care center in 15 days. *Building Design + Construction.* www.bdcnetwork.com/how-turn-high-school-patient-care-center-15-days

Centers for Disease Control and Prevention. (2020, March 26). Cleaning and disinfection for households. *CDC.* www.cdc.gov/coronavirus/2019-ncov/prevent-getting-sick/cleaning-disinfection.html

Education Reimagined. (2015). A transformational vision for education in the US. *Education Reimagined.* https://education-reimagined.org/wp-content/uploads/2019/01/Vision_Website.pdf

Kutylo, B. (2019, March 12). Start with teachers: Rethinking the change process in education. *Christensen Institute.* www.christenseninstitute.org/blog/why-reimaging-schools-means-reimagining-the-approach-to-change/?_sft_topics=policy,teacher-of-the-future

National Association of School Nurses. (2020, May 15). Interim guidance: Role of school nurse in return to school planning. *NASN.* https://higherlogicdownload.s3.amazonaws.com/NASN/3870c72d-fff9-4ed7-833f-215de278d256/UploadedImages/PDFs/COVID-19_Interim_Guidance_Role_of_the_School_Nurse_in_Return_to_School_Planning.pdf

NRT Bus Inc. (n.d.). Facts of bus riding. *NRT Bus Inc.* www.nrtbus.com/ parents/facts-of-bus-riding/

Stirman, S. W., Kimberly, J., Cook, N., Calloway, A., Castro, F., & Charns, M. (2012). The sustainability of new programs and innovations: A review of the empirical literature and recommendations for future research. *Implementation Science, 7*(1), 1–19. https://doi.org/10.1186/ 1748-5908-7-17

4 | Teaching as We Knew It

In This Chapter…

Introduction	75
Traditional Conventions	76
Narrative: *72 Hours: The Year with No Good-Byes*	78
Teaching, Learning, and the Schoolhouse	82
Narrative: *Adapting Instruction in the "New Normal"*	84
Human Connections	88
Narrative: *Relationships Can Thrive During a Crisis*	90
Leading for Tomorrow	96
References	90

 Introduction

Teachers, students, and parents had to navigate an educational system that looked very different from how it did a year ago. Regardless of the configurations of schooling that could be put in place for fall 2020 and beyond, teaching as we knew it changed. We all faced a new reality. Instruction, assessments, and other classroom conventions changed once schools shut down to stop the spread of COVID-19. In domino fashion, there were numerous changes that occurred as systems continued to seek new ways to educate students. This chapter examines the changes that occurred in teaching and learning, and the human connections needed between teachers, leaders, students, and their communities during these transitions.

Traditional Conventions

In moving through the challenges of this pandemic, many questions quickly emerged around traditional school conventions such as the calendars, number and length of school days, class schedules, and the use of assessments.

Use of Assessments

Early challenges for teachers were how to assess students and how to provide support. Schools districts across the country grappled with the balancing act on how to assess students while not being physically present to support them. In interviews with school districts, Sawchuk (2020) found that the district's primary interest was to provide students with feedback on assignments rather than a focus on grades. Primary concerns revolved around equity, students in poverty, the lack of digital access, and parents not being able to provide support to their children during the day.

Educators understood the need to provide feedback and stay connected to students even in a virtual environment. However, the traditional feedback and assessment framework relying mainly on tests no longer worked. According to Miller (2020), formatively assessing students in a virtual environment is challenging but is doable and effective. Considerations for creating a formative assessment system online include processes that:

1. have a clear purpose and routines using a few assessment tools;
2. collect data over time;
3. provide quality continuous feedback, make visual student connections using communication tools;
4. include ways to check on a student's well-being; and
5. use data to reflect on teaching practices.

In moving forward, policy-makers, school leaders and teachers will need to create greater clarity on the purposes and functions of standardized high-stakes testing as well as traditional in class assessments. The critical questions will be "Are systems assessing students *for* learning or merely of learning?"

High-stakes state-level testing systems and their use have been woven into the fabric of schools since before the No Child Left Behind Act (2002). Standardized tests impact students at almost every grade level and have often been inserted into teacher evaluation systems. Since the passage of the Every Student Succeeds Act of 2015, the amount of high-stakes testing required at the state and federal levels has been reduced. However, during the COVID-19 pandemic, states were exempted from federally required testing, bringing into question the future of federal and state accountability systems based primarily on high-stakes testing scores.

Use of Time and the School Calendar

Typically, the traditional conventions of schools are related to time linked to daily schedules and the school calendar. The start of the school day, students' schedules, structured curriculum, and specialized programs are all examples of conventions that require time. When schools moved to virtual environments, the use of time changed dramatically for conventions such as the start of the school day and student schedules. In addition, school was no longer associated only with what occurred within the daily schedule. The longstanding terms of "in school" versus "out of school" no longer described the school day.

Leaders and teachers continue to have concerns about "time" in a virtual environment given that student schedules were patchworked in a variety of ways that impacted learning. Research from the Northwest Evaluation Association (NWEA) predicted that students would return to school in fall 2020 with the COVID-19 slide, experiencing loss in at least two core subjects—language arts (30% loss) and up to a 50% loss in mathematics (Schaffhauser, 2020). Learning loss will have a substantial impact on the amount of time allocated to get students back to grade level.

Time is the most valuable resource as teachers and leaders unravel the complexities to address the wide range of learning gaps. Two areas of focus to best leverage the use of time include:

- looking at a different school calendar other than starting in the fall and ending in the spring with summers off; and,

- no longer defining the school day which is typically 8am to 3pm.

Teaching as We Knew It

A primary outcome of COVID-19 on the structure of school time will be the realization that time will no longer dictate school programming and student learning trajectories.

March 9 to March 12 started a very different journey for Dr. Mary Elizabeth Davis, the superintendent of Henry County Schools (HCS) located in McDonough, Georgia, and there was no looking back. As the eighth largest school district in Georgia, HCS serves approximately 43,000, K-12 students supported by more than 5,000 teachers, leaders, and staff.

Dr. Davis joined Henry County Schools in November 2017 and in that time period the district has seen an 11-point increase in state accountability metrics with more than half of the 50 schools posting double-digit gains including a steep increase in reading proficiency across the district in the early elementary grades. She led efforts with the Board of Education through the development of a Unified Governance Model which created alignment and focus for the organization from the boardroom to the classroom. Prior to HCS, Dr. Davis served as the Chief Academic Officer in Cobb County Schools, and she was previously an Assistant Superintendent for Curriculum & Instruction in Gwinnett County Public Schools. She began her career as a chemistry teacher in Fairfax, Virginia and is a 2015 graduate of the Broad Academy.

Dr. Davis shared the journey from making the decision to shut the schoolhouse doors to creating new system playbooks while fully embracing the importance of schools in the lives of students, families, and the community.

Mary Elizabeth Davis, Ph.D.
Superintendent
Henry County Schools
McDonough, GA

72 Hours: The Year with No Good-Byes

March 9, 2020 was the date of the monthly Board of Education meeting. It was a typical March evening with evidence of warmer temperatures and a sense of springtime in the air. March is always the point in the calendar year when the end of the school year becomes evident. The entire community's eyes are set on the pending spring break, and the promise of summer is in the air with all of the celebrations and rites of passage that accompany its arrival for students. We prepared for this March 9 Board meeting as we normally would, except for the fact that I had prepared to discuss the district's monitoring of COVID-19, but I also prepared reassuring words that there was no imminent threat to Henry County. At that time, I shared that public health officials deemed it to be safe to continue the typical operations of the school system and for students and employees to attend school regularly.

I jotted a note to myself on a Post-It note that I later found in my Board preparation notebook that read, "ask if BOE wants to shake hands." This note, of course, was a reminder to myself to ask the members of the Board of Education if they wanted to shake hands during the student recognition part of the board meeting. The question puzzled the board and without thinking twice, they did not hesitate to completely agree that, of course, they would shake kids' hands, take pictures with them, and celebrate their accomplishments. Incredible to think that this small thought for a change in typical behavior would become the first step in changing every system and process it takes to lead in public education. And now so many months later, the idea of it is almost ridiculous.

The New Journey Begins

On March 12, 2020, Henry County Schools made the decision to close schools for two weeks. I remember thinking this seemed so strange. We don't close schools often in Georgia, and we rarely have to manage inclement weather conditions so closing for a public health crisis seemed bizarre to announce.

Jump ahead just another 72 hours from Friday, March 13 to Monday, March 16, teachers across 50 schools moved their teaching from school classrooms to kitchen tables, living room floors, garages, and back porches. Printed packets, work texts, and media center materials were stuffed into the book bags of preK-2 students while 3rd–12th graders were encouraged to take home the district-issued devices, their chargers, and their personal belongings. Henry County Schools began with the plan to continue introducing new material and following the district pacing guides, but we did quickly adjust in response to screen fatigue and moved to priority standards and an adjusted schedule to reduce the amount of time teachers and students spent online.

Mobilizing the System

Some schools and teachers began the Remote Learning period by trying to follow the exact schedule of the typical school day, but we quickly learned that there needed to be modifications. As a system, we structured times for classes to meet digitally and collaborative planning with other teachers so times didn't overlap, and setting evening hours to accommodate families and their schedules. Our commitment remained that learning should continue, so school leaders conducted remote classroom visits, joined collaborative planning times with their teachers, and continued coaching and feedback cycles with teachers.

In 72 hours, teachers were able to establish a continuation of learning for students while the rest of the organization also rose to the challenge to rethink how departments were designed to support student learning—we had to rethink and reframe the work of central office staff as well. Social workers, counselors, and school psychologists began to partner with teachers to identify students who were not attending so that we could support any student with either barriers to access or with needs beyond academics that required support. School nutrition staff reinvented everything we have ever known about meal preparation, and we set up a curbside pick-up model that continued straight through the summer.

Our facilities and maintenance team members cleaned, sanitized, and secured every facility, bus, and district vehicle. For the most part, we closed the doors and locked them for what we thought would be two weeks. Of course, two weeks turned into two months, and all of the end-of-year processes and administrative procedures needed to be redesigned, communicated, and implemented at rapid-fire pace. Our schools became the key source for much needed

- food in the community for families in need of support; and,
- emotional and mental support for students and families.

As a system, we made it a top priority commitment to make education accessible to all students, attempting to ameliorate barriers to student success.

Pivoting to a Redesign

For an industry that has been historically known as bureaucratic, immobile, and difficult to change, in just 72 hours the entire schooling experience was upended and in another mere 72 hours, educators in Henry County managed to completely redesign the entire way that school is experienced, built stronger and more authentic relationships with parents, and rebuilt the foundation of a school system and its processes. This required three new key principles:

1. Clarity around the core business remaining intact—the core business of student learning.
2. Constant communication to principals, employees, and families— balancing information and inspiration and belief that we can do this.
3. Balancing the need to manage a response to a crisis while simultaneously leading an entire community one day at a time.

A New Hello

Without a doubt, leading through COVID-19 has reminded all of us the critical role that school plays in the lives of students, families, and the community. I believe that public education has remained the key unifying voice and force for communities that are traversing differences, realizing unresolved race conflicts, and navigating a worldwide health pandemic. Public education and public educators are by nature designed to open doors for kids, remove barriers for young people to reach their greatest potential, and to co-author stories that reflect challenges and triumphs. In a mere 72 hours, public education was pushed to its limits, and in Henry County, we rose to the challenge.

So, while we never got to say good-bye in the 2019–2020 school year the way we wish we could have, we never stopped looking for ways to make memories. Somehow the worries of how we would say good-bye became worries about how we would start anew to say hellos as we start the 2020–2021 school year.

Our Playbook

It was a long and grueling summer readying for fall 2020 as we envisioned multiple scenarios for the return or not of students. While it may seem like we had more than the 72 hours in March, we still had extensive reinventions and rebuilding to accomplish in order to make public education accessible during a worldwide pandemic.

Teaching as We Knew It

Henry County Schools has followed a model of producing district playbooks and then followed by local school playbooks (somewhat like workbooks) for detailed school planning within the parameters of the district.

At the point of this publication, we have a Facility Adaptation Playbook, a Keep Henry Healthy and COVID-19 Positive Case Protocol Playbook, a Remote Learning Playbook, and an On-Campus Learning Playbook. Each playbook meticulously provides clarity on the consistencies from school to school and is followed by the development of a local playbook for each of our 50 schools so that the customization necessary to build local routines and detailed preparations can be thoroughly considered.

The year of 2020–2021 will be like none other in our communities and in our schools, but we start the year knowing that we can do anything for kids and families even when we only have 72 hours to pull it off.

The 2020–2021 school year will be one like never before for Henry County Schools and systems across the country. Dr. Davis did not look back to say good-bye, but rather focused the system's efforts in moving forward in a systematic fashion by designing playbooks to guide the community, district systems, and schools as they navigated the unknown. Through her leadership, Dr. Davis and her school system are in a better place to say hello as teaching and learning resumes.

Teaching, Learning, and the Schoolhouse

One of the most significant questions that educators will need to ask is whether teaching and learning as we know it will permanently change because of what we learned when the schoolhouse doors closed. While moving to the virtual world had many things that were missing or inadequate (e.g., student access, inadequate curricular materials, etc.), the notion that the virtual environment is a viable model is now in the mainstream of education. No longer will online learning be called an alternative model; it will be considered a primary option for students to select as they navigate their learning journeys. For many teachers, teaching remotely

82

became complex. They needed to learn new skills and needed more resources, generally, to move their class content to the online environment. However, during this shift, teachers began to see a new and different opportunity to successfully engage their students.

Instructional Delivery

COVID-19 has changed every system in this country, creating a new normal. While students, parents, teachers, and leaders talk about getting back to the way things used to be, the rapid shifts in instructional design using virtual environments began to open new opportunities and innovations. The question of whether to implement a traditional or virtual instructional design was no longer reduced to a yes or no response. The new normal provides both options—creating greater bandwidth for meeting the needs of all children by expanding professional practices.

The move to virtual environments brought great insight into how teachers teach and how students learn. However, moving a virtual instructional design into a traditional framework was not easy and was often frustrating. While some teachers and students struggled when operating outside of the traditional framework, others were engaged and flourished. It became readily apparent that no one way is effective for every teacher and student.

While districts made valiant efforts to prepare teachers for the shift, teachers struggled and often leveraged their experiences from a traditional setting to engage students online with mixed results. According to Dede (2020), "the most difficult part of surmounting the challenges of remote learning is unlearning the psychological and cultural assumptions that impede us from using this opportunity to improve our practice" (para. 11). Virtual learning in a digital world will require new constructs for instructional design and delivery based on the new needs of learners. Embedded in the success of a virtual component beyond COVID-19 is an understanding of how students learn differently.

COVID-19 created the opportunity to move teaching beyond the schoolhouse as described by Mr. Jeff C. McCoy, the Associate Superintendent for Academics of Greenville County Schools (GCS) located in Greenville, South Carolina. GCS serves 76,999 K-12 students supported by nearly 6,000 teachers and 10,000 employees. Mr. McCoy has served

Teaching as We Knew It

the Greenville County Schools in the roles of a school International Baccalaureate Coordinator, an Instructional Technology Specialist, Distance Learning Coordinator, Director of Instructional Technology, and Director of Academic Innovation and Technology.

Mr. McCoy, in his Narrative, spoke to future instructional program changes, stressing the need for adaptability in a world that will continue to shift. He projected there will be a substantive impact on current instructional delivery models as a result of emerging virtual environments and significant changes in traditional instructional structures.

Mr. Jeff C. McCoy
Associate Superintendent for Academics
Greenville County Schools
Greenville, SC

Adapting Instruction in the "New Normal"

Several weeks before COVID-19 shut down school systems across the country, I was discussing with colleagues how far we had come as a district when it came to instructional strategies and student engagement. The last several years have been good to Greenville County Schools as test scores continued to rise, and teachers began embracing innovative strategies for teaching and learning. Our goal of moving away from lecturing and more into collaborative learning was finally becoming the norm instead of the exception. When COVID-19 hit and schools shut down, it was several weeks into the pandemic when we started realizing we would not be returning to normal. It quickly became evident that COVID-19 was going to vastly change how we do business.

I remembered sitting on my patio on a Zoom conference with my staff when someone asked how we were going to modify our instructional strategies in a world where social distancing was going to probably be the new normal. I remember vividly thinking that everything we worked so hard for the last several years was basically going to be undone. All our amazing teachers who embraced the new learning strategies were going to have to adapt again back to the old way of doing things—a way that we already knew was not effective.

84

We realized immediately that our instructional strategies involving group work and collaboration may have to be temporarily suspended. However, we also realized that our students were already doing group work and collaborating with each other and they were not even in the same physical space! While educators' hearts all over the country were hurting because the soft skills taught in person every day seemed impossible to continue, it was also a great time for us to rethink how we were doing things. We also realized that some of the soft skills students have to learn for remote learning will be critical life skills in the future in the world of virtual meetings. Education has needed a disruptive force for some time now. While we have made many changes the last few years that greatly benefited our students, the COVID-19 pandemic forced us out of our comfort zone and into a world our students were much more prepared for than we were.

Educators are perhaps the most adaptable people in the world. In less than 48 hours, our teachers made the shift from traditional face-to-face teaching to virtual teaching. Many of them had no training to make this massive shift. While our e-learning implementation was not perfect, it was successful given the two-day timeframe we had to completely redesign how we teach and how students learned. Throughout the last several months, several key insights emerged. As a system, we learned:

- **The move to e-learning forced us to rethink how students learn.** The Greenville County Schools has prided itself on being a personalized learning district. In reality, our teachers are still learning how to personalize instruction in the classroom because it is incredibly difficult. However, when we did a focus group with students, it was surprising how many of them said they loved e-learning because they were able to learn at their own pace and even explore things they would not have been able to do in a face-to-face classroom. While there were mixed results (some students loving e-learning, some students hating it), it helped us realize that as far as we have come in education, we still have a somewhat of a "one size fits all" model.

- **High school will most likely never look the same.** After our focus groups with students, senior leadership quickly began to realize high school does not have to be the same in the future. Whether another COVID-19 strikes or another disruption, we know now we

Teaching as We Knew It

can successfully teach students without them being on campus every single day. We are already beginning to think differently about high school. Could it be set up like a college where students only have to come in certain days of the week? We created a virtual program in a matter of weeks which we plan to keep going long after COVID-19 finally exits. This option will be for students who prefer online learning over face-to-face in grades K-12.

- **Instructional strategies will survive.** Social distancing is not ideal in a classroom. We recognize we may have to implement temporarily some strategies that are not ideal, but they will hopefully be a short-term solution. Instead of getting into groups and huddling up to complete projects, students may very well have to complete those projects "virtually" in Google Classroom and collaborate on virtual platforms versus in person—even though they may be sitting six feet away from each other. While sitting six feet away or collaborating virtually with classmates may not be ideal, I believe these practices teach students skills they are going to need in this global society we now live in. Companies are no longer requiring employees to be in a physical office space. Many are scattered around the world and collaborate virtually on platforms daily. This is a critical skill in the age we now live in. Students practicing virtual collaboration is not a bad thing, and it is a good stop-gap measure in a world where we may have to do social distancing.

- **E-learning doesn't have to be second rate**. For many traditional educators, you will still often hear the phrase "virtual instruction is not as good as face-to-face." I believe that was probably true at one time, but we are fast moving out of the reality of that statement. That statement is also made by people who never experienced virtual learning as a student. Times have changed, and students have changed. Many of our students said they liked e-learning better because it gave them the flexibility to learn at their own pace and provided them with a flexible schedule. As our teachers get better at designing online content, I believe many of our students will prefer this method of learning over the traditional face-to-face learning model. We have already received feedback from parents and students on our e-learning implementation and have already begun changing some of the things that were not as positive for our students.

I believe in socialization as much as I believe that some students learn better in an online environment; however, looking forward, schools must be able to offer both online and face-to-face instruction seamlessly. COVID-19 has quickly made the blended environment a necessary reality and that is the silver lining of this pandemic.

Predicated on collaboration and group work, Mr. McCoy provided insight into how learning in a virtual environment can work in tandem with in-person learning strategies. Changing our assumptions will take time and ongoing professional learning to understand the new work of teaching.

The New Work of Teaching

The shift to online instruction models necessitates changes in our thinking about effective teaching and the traditional work of teachers. In the future, class loads and teaching schedules may no longer be the currency for teacher work as online instruction looks substantially different than being in the front of a classroom. Information is not scarce today—in fact, we probably suffer from information overload. The new role of teachers is to help students seek and authenticate information by developing their abilities to ask questions, apply new information, think critically, solve problems, and make informed judgments. Table 4.1 illustrates the differences between traditional and virtual teacher work models.

While these traditional conventions are shifting due to the design of virtual environments, the largest impact on the work of teachers will be driven by a new understanding of what students should know and be able to do to be successful in their world. With the changes made in response to COVID-19, teachers and leaders are now more aware of how the current generation accesses their learning and sees themselves differently, perhaps not fitting into the traditional instructional setting.

Teachers now see themselves as no longer relegated to the front of a classroom or confined to a school building. Teaching is now freed to occur anywhere or at any time. However, regardless of place, teaching and

Table 4.1 Traditional and virtual teacher work models

Teachers in a traditional teacher work model	Teachers in a virtual teacher work model
Give information in the class.	Create questions and frame problems in class.
Give homework to learn more information.	Design assignments for students collectively to discuss new information.
Review homework in the classroom and give more information.	Discuss and collaborate on applications.
Administer tests to demonstrate mastery of content.	Differentiate ways that students demonstrate mastery of content and skills through reflection and application of skills learned.

learning remains a human endeavor that requires social interactions and connections that must remain whether in person or in a virtual environment.

Human Connections

Education has always been grounded in the relationships between adults and students and a caring teacher is the cornerstone of teaching. Students and teachers spend hundreds of hours each year together, and the relationships formed are the catalyst for student success. Today, most remember school by recalling the positive impact a teacher or teachers had on both their learning and life growing up. As schools move forward in developing new designs using digital tools, maintaining and supporting the human capital between students and teachers must be at the center of the work.

When people feel connected, they feel safe to freely share ideas, to seek clarity, and to offer solutions to thorny issues. However, feeling connected in schools goes deeper. Positive relationships cannot flourish in an environment where people feel disconnected or disenfranchised from the system. As teachers and leaders build new instructional systems the question that needs to be answered is how to build human capital with teachers, students, and parents in a virtual world.

Connecting in a Virtual World

Throughout COVID-19 conventional communication patterns and in-person interactions occurred remotely through digital tools such as Skype, Zoom, Google Hangout, and faceless communication through email, phone, and instant messenger on Facebook. Staying connected remotely requires new approaches. When schools closed, teachers were the first to respond by staying connected to their students. In a virtual world, teachers have been adamant that staying connected to their students must be a priority. Court (2020) suggests that teachers can ask themselves these questions to guide to develop relationships with students in a virtual classroom:

1. Do you know this student's name and face?
2. Have you had contact with this student since we started remote learning?
3. Have you sent this student a personal, positive message in the past week?
4. Are you aware of any barriers that this student is facing while trying to participate in remote learning?
5. Can you name two non-academic facts about this student?
6. Do you know this student's family story?

The response from teachers on creating relationships with students virtually is mixed: some have said it can be done successfully while others have vowed it will never work.

Dr. Susan Stancil, principal of Dove Creek Elementary School (Statham, GA), shared in her Narrative, the work needed to keep connected with their students, their parents, and each other once their school closed. Dove Creek Elementary School serves 605 K-5 students supported by 47 teachers and 31 support staff. Prior to opening Dove Creek Elementary School, Dr. Stancil was the principal of Malcom Bridge Elementary School, which was named a Blue-Ribbon Lighthouse School in 2016.

During this time of turmoil, Dr. Stancil described and illustrated the importance of relationships. She understood the work that needed to be accomplished and focused on supporting the faculty and staff who put forth their best efforts every day as they navigated the turbulence.

Teaching as We Knew It

Susan Stancil, Ph.D.
Principal
Dove Creek Elementary School
Oconee County School District
Statham, GA

Relationships Can Thrive During a Crisis

Many factors contribute to a student's academic performance, but teachers matter most. A dual role of the principal is to hire the very best staff possible and to focus on building a positive and healthy culture that inspires trust and relationships. Relationships matter.

At Dove Creek Elementary School, our number one priority since we opened two years ago was to create an environment that was positive, welcoming, and where parents would be proud to send their children. Before COVID-19 and moving into the digital environment, you could come through our car rider line on any given day to find music playing and teachers dancing to welcome our students. Once inside, students were met with smiling faces and teachers who knew them by name. Strong connections, positive relationships, and an amazing environment were our top priorities every day. Everyone at our school is proud to be part of what we call the dragon family.

So, how did we continue once we had to be away from our students and teachers, separated from each other? Here are some of our strategies:

- Daily morning announcements were recorded by the principal and sent electronically so students and parents could hear a message to get their day started. Our assistant principal recited the pledge of allegiance and held a moment of silence, similar to our normal routine. We posted videos of students telling the "dragon" joke of the day.

- Similar to our beginning of the school year video, we produced two special music videos to keep our students and families feeling positive while we were apart. One video was set to the tune of "My House" by Flo Rida, but we changed the words to welcome students into "Our House" as we danced with our families in our own living rooms and

90

at our front doors, and then students joined in with their own video version of "Our House" (both available on YouTube).

- We used an ABC Countdown with our students for the last 26 days of school including activities such as a virtual field day, rock 'n' roll day complete with an online musical production from our fifth-grade chorus students, online author visits, etc.

- Since one of the most successful themed days was letter F – Fine Arts Day, our art teacher challenged families to recreate famous works of art and share them on our social media sites. This outreach was featured on the front page of the local newspaper.

- Our faculty and staff held a Dragon Parade lasting over four hours while making stops in the neighborhoods where our students live. Our staff showed up with their cars decked with balloons, streamers, inflatable dragons, signs, and more. Our students and families participated by decking out their driveways and yards. Everyone was dressed from head-to-toe in green—our signature color.

- A teacher was assigned to manage our social media outreach to share these exciting events and to post news daily to keep everyone engaged and connected.

While it was certainly important to engage our students and families, it was also critical to keep out faculty and staff connected and appreciated. We created structures including:

- Weekly virtual faculty meetings.
- Weekly virtual grade level meetings.
- Staff Appreciation Week: This was to highlight and boost morale for the entire staff. Our PTO delivered yard signs to every staff member's home. The signs said: "A Superhero Lives Here." The PTO raised money to give an Amazon gift card to every staff member.
- The assistant principal and I held a drive-through pizza party at a local establishment where teachers could drive through and have lunch on us!

The connections that were made during COVID-19 will continue to help us as we move forward. As parents assumed the role of teacher during the pandemic and tried to keep instruction going at home, they began to realize that teaching is very hard work! Based on social media reports, it appears that the coronavirus pandemic has led parents to develop a greater recognition for teachers and the teaching profession once they had to start facilitating their child's learning from home.

Parents with two or more children on different learning levels and at different ages were having to "differentiate" and "individualize" instruction for the first time. This gave parents a whole new respect for what our teachers do every day. The daily online assignments and virtual meetings that teachers had with their students also gave parents a closer look at how creative our teachers are and how they go above and beyond in everything they do. This newfound appreciation for the education profession will continue positively to impact our school as we return to normal.

We feel like we thrived and learned a lot during the pandemic. As we move forward, we will build professional learning for flipped classrooms and digital learning into our yearly plans to make teachers (and students) more comfortable in a virtual environment. We will expand on what worked well and will be better prepared for possible school closures in the future.

In moving forward, we will focus on providing the support needed as we build relationships, and we will:

- build relationships with students and families early to ensure they know and feel loved by all staff that are currently serving them;
- make sure that students (and parents) are comfortable using the technology outside of the classroom setting;
- increase communication with our families to ensure they are constantly aware of our processes, procedures, and learning models in the event that we have another school closure.

As a school leader, my number one priority has not changed. Hire the very best staff and put them in spots where they can best shine. Also, a positive culture and relationships must always be at the forefront. The foundation of culture and relationships must be in place so your school can withstand any disturbance that disrupts schools from serving their students and families.

Dr. Stancil emphasized the importance of building relationships not only between students and teachers but also between leaders, teachers, and parents. In her school, the challenges of COVID-19 were much easier to address given their culture of trust and care.

Additionally, building relationships and keeping the human element between teachers and leaders cannot be overlooked in a virtual space. Teachers and leaders want to work with colleagues they know personally and professionally, who they can trust, and who they have enjoyed positive relationships with. Building relations in a virtual space can be done. Arruda (2018) promotes that building professional relationships online requires three considerations: "transparency, likability and credibility. Transparency lets people get to know you, while likability reflects their interest in you and credibility builds trust" (para. 3). Similarly, leaders need to build relationships differently as well and develop new ways to stay connected. Hickman and Robinson (2020) suggests that leaders purposefully stay connected and engaged through virtual conversations that include:

- role and relationship development;
- quick connect;
- check-in;
- developmental coaching; and,
- progress review.

(Hickman and Robinson, 2020, para. 10)

A longstanding priority for schools has been to engage parents and guide them in helping support their children. Like teachers, supportive parents as well as advocates are essential for students to be successful in school. "Schools—if only by necessity—must support families in their role as educators. Parents' love for their children is the single greatest—and most underutilized—natural resource in education" (Seale, 2020, para. 8). With COVID-19 and school from home, the disparity in the support of students by parents and family members has become very clear. It will be critical for leaders and teachers to understand the family dynamics within their districts to provide additional support to meet the diverse needs of families.

Cultivating Social Capital Virtually

The COVID-19 pandemic caused a significant disruption, raising concerns about student isolation and the sense of belonging—all leading to the erosion of the social capital important to a school's success. Specifically, the question remains whether schools will lose their social capital as a result of interactions occurring online. Albeit situated in higher education, a study by Kent et al. (2019) found a positive association between offline social capital and online learning. They found at the community level that online learning compliments building offline social capital. The most significant takeaway from this study for the K-12 sector is the need to determine how online learning builds and supports social capital found typically in the physical school building.

Today, much can be learned about building social capital especially as schools prepare for future disruptions. The overall findings from Pitas and Ehmer's (2020) study about social capital and the impact of COVID-19 on it, indicates that expanding a stronger focus on social networks now and in preparing for the future are needed. Pitas and Ehmer recommend, specifically that:

1. Individuals, communities, and government institutions should focus on building and maintaining a variety of social ties during the present crisis. Social capital, of all forms, will increase adherence to, and improve the efficacy of, physical distancing and other protective behaviors. [...]
2. Digital mediated communication tools must play a larger role in generating social capital during the current pandemic. Although the effects of media–based social capital are less understood, digital and other mediated forms of communication must be utilized as a means of creating and nurturing social connections. [...]
3. Must learn from the effects of the current crisis and prepare for future disaster scenarios. The impacts of COVID-19 on social capital, and the role of social capital in responding to COVID-19, must be the subject of rigorous, ongoing research.

(Pitas & Ehmer, 2020, pp. 2–3)

The heart and soul of schools is driven by the social interactions that occur daily.

Understanding the value of social capital in bringing about stability in the midst of change is what will keep schools balanced and lessen opportunity gaps caused by an inability to engage in a physical setting.

Reestablishing Equilibrium

School systems, families, and students have experienced great disequilibrium of schedules (work, school, life) as children attended school in their living rooms and other places where the Internet was available. Parents assumed new roles by having the responsibility to monitor and support their children's learning at home. The parents who sheltered in place with their children at home became teachers in addition to their roles as parents. For other parents who were working outside the home, the involvement in their children's learning became challenging and often inconsistent. For students, the learning options were often relegated to sitting in cars in a parking lot, finding open libraries and seeking access anywhere the Internet was available. Everything familiar about going to school was toppled.

Similarly, teachers had limited instructional options as they scrambled to move into a virtual environment. The fast-paced professional learning on teaching in virtual environments provided only an entree into best practices resulting in high levels of frustration as teachers sought to engage their students without being physically with them. Moreover, teachers struggled and sought ways to maintain relationships they knew to be essential to their work. Teachers with children assumed the dual role as a parent responsible for teaching their own children. Balancing multiple responsibilities became overwhelming.

School systems are frenetically working on a variety of plans as they seek to return to a state of normalcy and equilibrium knowing that it will not be the same as before COVID-19. While digital tools and platforms have the capacity to replicate classroom spaces and to move instruction, the roles of teachers and parents are being reimagined to support personal and professional responsibilities, build social capital, and bridge new designs between the school and parents.

Creating balance after the intense redesign and delivery of online instruction will bring a new normal to schools and how they function. No longer will the traditions of the mainstream school be built on Monday through Friday schedules with set daily school hours. No longer will you see all students enrolled in the school walking through the doors at the beginning of the day. Given social distancing and online learning as schools move forward, new ways to connect in a virtual world will evolve.

However, not all traditional ways of connecting with people will disappear with the new normal. Everyone—adults and children—need balance in their lives and schools are foundational in making that happen. They, along with their communities, will cultivate social capital so teachers, students, and leaders can rebound after the physical isolation of moving through the COVID-19 pandemic and beyond.

Leading for Tomorrow

Education faced a new reality as the delivery of programs shifted when the school doors closed. Teaching and learning as we knew it no longer existed, and the school supports typically provided to students were in flux and required:

- rethinking the use of state and federal requirements such as high-stakes testing;
- modifying and rewriting contracts and policies to define the work of teachers in non-traditional classroom settings;
- establishing a new equilibrium to the pace of learning and the work of students and teachers (i.e., work schedules and calendars);
- adapting the innovations made in virtual instructional programs rather than reverting back to a traditional program.

In moving forward, a new normal will be created from the lessons learned during this pandemic and the willingness of teachers and leaders to seek and maintain new solutions that align with and bring a semblance of a new equilibrium.

References

Arruda, W. (2018, November 9). How to build real relationships in the virtual world. *Forbes*. www.forbes.com/sites/williamarruda/2018/11/09/how-to-build-real-relationships-in-the-virtual-world/#5738610b5751

Court, B. (2020, April 9). Remote relationship mapping: Don't let students go unnoticed during COVID-19. *EAB*. https://eab.com/insights/expert-insight/student-success/remote-relationship-mapping-dont-let-students-go-unnoticed-during-covid-19/

Dede, C. (2020, May 6). Remote learning and stone soup. *Learning Policy Institute*. https://learningpolicyinstitute.org/blog/remote-learning-and-stone-soup

Every Student Succeeds Act of 2015, Pub. L. No. 114–95 § 114 Stat. 1177 (2015–2016).

Hickman, A., & Robinson, J. (2020, May 1). 5 facts about engagement and remote workers. *Gallup*. www.gallup.com/workplace/309521/facts-engagement-remote-workers.aspx

Kent, C., Rechavi, A., & Rafaeli, S. (2019). The relationship between offline social capital and online learning interactions. *International Journal of Communication*, *13*, 1186–1211. https://ijoc.org/index.php/ijoc/article/view/10213/2590

Miller, A. (2020, April 7). Formative assessment in distance learning. *Edutopia*. www.edutopia.org/article/formative-assessment-distance-learning

No Child Left Behind (NCLB) Act of 2001, Pub. L. No. 107–110, § 115, Stat. 1425 (2001).

Pitas, N., & Ehmer, C. (2020). Social capital in the response to COVID-19. *American Journal of Health Promotion*, 1–3. https://doi.org/10.1177/0890117120924531

Sawchuk, S. (2020, April 1). Grading students during the coronavirus crisis: What's the right call? *Education Week*. www.edweek.org/ew/articles/2020/04/01/grading-students-during-the-coronavirus-crisis-whats.html

Schaffhauser, D. (2020, April 21). Research: Coronavirus learning loss could put some students behind a full year. *The Journal*. https://thejournal.com/articles/2020/04/21/research-coronavirus-learning-loss-could-put-some-students-behind-a-full-year.aspx

Seale, C. (2020, May 19). Parent involvement has always mattered. Will the COVID-19 pandemic finally make this the new normal in K-12 education? *Forbes*. www.forbes.com/sites/colinseale/2020/05/19/parent-involvement-has-always-mattered-will-the-covid-19-pandemic-finally-make-this-the-new-normal-in-k-12-education/#45a92d5e5e46

5 Supporting Social and Emotional Needs

In This Chapter...

Introduction	99
Student Growth and Social Development	100
Narrative: *Supporting Student Social Emotional Wellness During a Time of Isolation*	103
Social Dynamics of Schools	106
Narrative: *Lessons Learned While Navigating the Unknown*	111
New Thinking Moving Forward	114
Narrative: *We Really Did Own It*	117
Leading for Tomorrow	122
References	123

Introduction

At birth, socialization begins through human interactions with parents, siblings, and other relatives and grows as children's social networks expand. Across the lifespan, people are socialized in a variety of ways through countless interactions and affiliations with people and organizations such as churches, daycares, schools, and community clubs and organizations.

Developing social skills continues to be a core K-12 responsibility along with academic growth. When the schoolhouse doors closed, concerns emerged with supporting student academic progress as well as social development. This chapter examines student growth and social development, the social dynamics of schools, and the new thinking needed as schools plan to move forward.

Student Growth and Social Development

Understanding the processes by which students gain confidence in who they are, how they positively interact with other students and adults, and how they manage their emotions is woven into the foundation of education. Educational organizations such as the National Education Association (NEA, 2018) understand and support the role of teachers in not only academic success but also the essential role they play in developing skills that are critical to being a good student, citizen, and worker.

Importance of Social Skill Development

While not viewed or measured in the same way as academic skill development, developing social skills in schools is among the most important functions leading to student success. The impact of social and emotional learning is not new but research continues to substantiate its positive relationship to school success (Mahoney et al., 2018) and long-term psychological well-being (Cristóvão et al., 2017). A meta-analysis of the research illustrated that social and emotional learning positively impacts a student's attitudes about themselves, improves attitudes and behaviors while decreasing negative behaviors, and improves academic achievement (Durlak & Mahoney, 2019). As educators and leaders work through the current and future issues resulting from COVID-19, it becomes even more important to understand the dynamics of social development.

As students move from being at home or from childcare centers and into kindergarten, their social development is changing rapidly, especially as they spend more time with other children and adults. According to SCAN (n.d.), by five years old social development rises to new levels and it is normal for children to:

- Thrive on friendships
- Want to please friends, as well as be more like their friends
- Begin to recognize power in relationships, as well as the larger community

Supporting Social and Emotional Needs

- Recognize and fear bullies or display bully-like behavior themselves,
- As early as 10, children begin rejecting parents' opinion of friends and certain behaviors—this is a normal step, but can be especially frustrating for parents.

(SCAN, n.d., para. 47–51)

As students grow and move into different stages of their lives and school grade levels, the need for social development continues. Social and emotional needs may be at the highest during adolescence because young adults are:

- Developing the ability to reevaluate their emotional responses to social situations,
- Taking on more adult roles and responsibilities,
- Improving their capacity to understand and engage in complex social interactions,
- Forming new types of relationships (romantic, professional, deeper friendships),
- Increasingly sensitive to evaluation from others,
- Understanding themselves and how they fit within larger social contexts,
- Shifting behavior based on peer influence and adult presence,
- Navigating cultural influences and societal expectations.

(Alliance for Excellent Education, 2018, p. 1)

Developing social skills is directly impacted by what occurs in schools, providing educators with a critical responsibility to help students navigate the numerous new interactions they experience through their school years.

Role of the School

For many, the schoolhouse is one of the first structured environments where students interact with other children outside of their families and friends and begin to develop the social skills they need to interact with others. While some students begin this process early in their development by enrolling in daycare centers and preK, others experience a structured environment with other children for the first time in kindergarten. Evidence points to the importance of social development so students have the ability to positively engage with others and exhibit self-control in different environments (Moffitt et al., 2011).

John Dewey, at the turn of the 19th century, outlined the perspective that is still applicable today, 120 years later. Dewey, in his 1897 creed, summarized "that education... is a process of living and not a preparation for future living" (p. 78). Too often, teachers and school leaders respond to student experiences and behaviors by indicating that it will be different in the "real" world. The term "real" may be inappropriate to use in schools and with children as their experiences are very real and are critical to their development. For students, being in a classroom and interacting with peers is the real world. Children take away invaluable lessons from their school experiences as they develop social and emotional skills.

On many occasions, the role of the school in developing social skills has come into question. The prevalent perspective exists that schools are responsible for learning, and that parents have the responsibility of developing appropriate social skills. However, in reality, schools assume tremendous responsibility for supporting the social and emotional development of children's social skills. This responsibility, combined with today's increased social challenges and demands on parents, now requires schools to partner with parents and collectively develop the social skills students need (National Association of School Psychologists, n.d.).

Social and emotional learning is at the center of the efforts of Superintendent Dr. Armand Pires of the Medway Public Schools (MPS), and he understands the need to focus systematically on student well-being. MPS is a suburban system that serves approximately 2,178 preK-12 students supported by 265 teachers and 100 staff. Dr. Pires has served the Medway Public Schools for more than a decade as a principal, assistant superintendent, and superintendent for the last five years.

In his Narrative, Dr. Pires presented how his system used a framework to support the social and emotional wellness of students during COVID-19, and how this framework could propel support in the future. Critical to their success was developing and implementing a systems approach addressing all stakeholders using multiple levels of intervention.

Armand Pires, Ph.D.
Superintendent
Medway Public Schools
Medway, MA

Supporting Student Social Emotional Wellness During a Time of Isolation

The Medway Public Schools is a small suburban district with four schools and approximately 2,200 students. The focus of the district is guided by the Strategic Plan, *Excellence for All: A Medway Mindset, 2019–2024*. Our Strategic Plan includes social and emotional wellness as a goal, and comprehensive wellness as a core value.

The COVID-19 health pandemic left all of us feeling out of balance as we moved from a traditional school experience in early March to a fully online educational experience that persisted through the end of the 2019–2020 school year. The school closure came with little warning and almost no planning. Certainly, it seemed impossible that we would be out of school for the remainder of the school year when the initial close occurred.

Relying on the framework of our Strategic Plan to guide decisions in this time of crisis was key to ensuring that we continued the critical work of the district. We were guided by our core values. We focused our initial planning around two primary areas: mitigating educational regression, and supporting students' social emotional wellness. We believe that these two areas are critical to students' success and that it is not possible to be successful in one area without the other. As a result, we focused our planning efforts to ensure that we were able to effectively meet the needs of our students both educationally and from a social emotional frame.

Using a Framework
The *Multi-Tiered Systems of Support (MTSS) Framework* developed by the Massachusetts Department of Elementary and Secondary Education (n.d.) was used as a framework for planning. This model, more commonly known as *Response to Intervention* (RTI), provides an organizing framework to plan and act on the needs of students. The MTSS includes three tiers of support, which build on one another.

Tier 1: Supports available to all students through a general education program.

Tier 2: In addition to Tier 1 supports, supports students who need additional practice and support, can occur in small groups.

Tier 3: Intensive support that is focused on individuals or very small groups of students.

Applying a Tiered Approach

As we began planning around student needs in the area of social and emotional wellness, we anticipated an increased need to view supports provided remotely as different from usual supports. We organized and planned with the following in mind:

- Our Tier 1 approaches might not be effective or sufficient to support students remotely.
- Students who were well-served by Tier 1 supports might need enhanced supports due to increased anxiety or trauma.
- Students already receiving supports via Tier 2, might require even more intensive supports.
- The number of students requiring intensive individualized support would likely increase.

Through the planning process, we identified available social-emotional and academic supports for students during the time of school closure. We also considered what additional supports were necessary to ensure that we were meeting the needs of *all* students and identified key personnel and programs available to provide these services. Throughout the school closure, we reviewed feedback from our professional staff and adjusted, as necessary, to ensure alignment with targeted needs. A few of the approaches, organized by MTSS Tiers, are presented:

Tier 1:
- All students received live, synchronous instruction by their teachers for 4–7 hours per week.
- Elementary classes were divided into two groups to provide increased attention to each learner within the virtual environment.

Supporting Social and Emotional Needs

- We continued to use Responsive Classroom Morning Meeting (Responsive Classroom, 2016).
- Students at the secondary level participated in "office hours" for regular checks-in with teachers.
- Secondary students completed a required online program addressing stress and prevention efforts.
- A website that collated mental health resources for parents was developed.

Tier 2:

- Newly established supports were identified for students struggling with behavioral or social emotional challenges during remote learning.
- Professional staff members followed up with all students/families who were not participating in remote learning.
- Small groups were created to support academic and social emotional learning.
- A mental health referral service hotline to our families was publicized.

Tier 3:

- Specialized services were continued via remote learning model.
- Internal staff provided access to additional intensive behavioral supports as needed.
- At family request, access to behavioral consultant services were provided.
- A community partnership provided increased access to mental health counseling resources, via telehealth.

Moving into the Future through Coordinated Planning

The impact of the COVID-19 public health crisis provides both an opportunity and necessity for innovation and focus in schools as never before. During this time of disruption, the importance of both student academic learning and social emotional wellness are clear and require coordinated planning to achieve related goals. Successful support for students and families within the framework of remote learning relies heavily on the developed relationships between teachers and students. To foster these relationships, it is critical that planning for learning during this time of disruption focus on opportunities for students and teachers to engage in ways that build trusting and effective relationships. These experiences must include personalization of services and include live full-class, small group, and individual interactions with students.

As we consider this public health crisis, and prepare for a school year that will likely include more closures and students again participating in remote learning, it is critical that we support the continued connection between teacher and student for both in-person and remote learning experiences.

Dr. Pires provided a framework to support students as they moved through stages of social development during this time of instructional transitions. In his district, developing strong teacher and student relationships guided decisions to ensure social growth leading to academic success.

The importance of teaching social and emotional skills in schools has emerged from those who study child development, education, and health (Jones et al., 2017). Schools across the country have engaged in initiatives looking at non-cognitive development that is broadly defined under Social and Emotional Learning (SEL). Implementing SEL is becoming a critical movement for schools across the country during this pandemic as they address the needs of children and adults in the system.

Social Dynamics of Schools

Educators across the country understand the important role they play in helping students develop the social and emotional skills they need to be productive and successful. Moving forward as more is learned about the impact of COVID-19, school SEL programs will become even more critical to the support of teachers, students, and members of the community.

Social and Emotional Learning

Social and Emotional Learning (SEL) is an umbrella to a wide range of social skill development spanning from birth all the way through adulthood.

Supporting Social and Emotional Needs

According to the Collaborative for Academic, Social, and Emotional Learning (CASEL), SEL "is the process through which children and adults understand and manage emotions, set and achieve positive goals, feel and show empathy for others, establish and maintain positive relationships, and make responsible decisions" (CASEL, n.d.a, para. 1). Mahoney et al. (2018) share that "SEL is neither a fad nor a flash in the pan but represents a useful way to improve students' social and emotional skills, which are associated with several positive behavioral and academic outcomes" (p. 22).

Research studies highlight the importance SEL plays in a student's social, emotional, and cognitive growth. Overall, students in SEL programs experienced greater academic gains than students not enrolled in SEL programs (Wiglesworth et al., 2016). SEL is not a curriculum, and its overall aims are to create opportunities that enhance "students' capacity to integrate skills, attitudes, and behaviors to deal effectively and ethically with daily tasks and challenges" (CASEL, n.d.b, para. 1). CASEL (n.d.b) identified five competency areas within a SEL framework, found in Table 5.1.

Table 5.1 CASEL competency areas

Competency	Definition
Self-awareness	● Accurately recognize one's own emotions, thoughts, and values and how they influence behavior.
Self-management	● Successfully regulate one's emotions, thoughts, and behaviors in different situations ● Effectively manage stress, control impulses, and motivate oneself.
Social awareness	● Take the perspective of and empathize with others, including those from diverse backgrounds and cultures.
Relationship skills	● Establish and maintain healthy and rewarding relationships with diverse individuals and groups.
Responsible decision-making	● Make constructive choices about personal behavior and social interactions based on ethical standards, safety concerns, and social norms.

Adapted from CASEL (n.d.b).

The COVID-19 pandemic creates a tremendous responsibility for schools to respond to the social and emotional needs of not only students but also adults. Building on the knowledge from SEL can help guide schools through the social emotional challenges created by COVID-19.

The Social and Emotional Impact of COVID-19

Providing services to mitigate the impact of COVID-19 was a daunting responsibility. While much of the focus was about the physical safety of students, teachers, and all who would re-enter the school building, a backdrop of an emotional impact became increasingly apparent. When schools closed, many of the social and emotional supports for students diminished and even disappeared despite tremendous efforts by schools to maintain a level of support through virtual platforms. Students, teachers, and staff were hurting from the isolation necessitated by social distancing, from disrupted routines, and from other worries related to safety, health, finances, etc.

The Needs of Adults. In the rapid response to meet the social and emotional demands of children to stay healthy, the needs of adults may have been overlooked. Addressing the stress and anxiety levels of teachers as they navigated meeting a changing teaching and learning environment became an emerging priority. Garcia and Mirra (2020) aptly explain, "A reconfigured school cannot function effectively without the energy, ingenuity and love imparted by teachers" (para. 12). In a recent survey (Cipriano & Brackett, 2020), teachers described their feelings as a result of COVID-19 as *anxious, fearful, worried, overwhelmed,* and *sad.* A comparison of responses pre-COVID-19 illustrated the top emotions were *frustrated, overwhelmed, stressed, tired,* and *happy.* Overall, there exists a pattern that teachers are frustrated with new emotions emerging from COVID-19, and require added social emotional support.

Teachers are worried about whether they can do their job and balance all of the demands on them as teachers and as parents. In a *USA Today* poll, 83% of teachers indicated that they were having a harder time doing their job, and two-thirds said they had to work more than usual (Page, 2020). Furthermore two-thirds indicated that they have not been able to do their job properly since starting to teach in a virtual environment and one in five teachers indicated that they will likely leave the profession.

Supporting Social and Emotional Needs

The need for social and emotional support for teachers has been growing and now leaders must create the conditions that promote the sense of emotional safety and social connections that adults, like students, will need to work and learn productively. Supporting a vibrant and engaged faculty must be at the center of schools successfully moving past COVID-19. Velez (2020) provides recommendations for school leaders as they plan the next transitions back into the schoolhouse:

- Involve employees in the process of creating safe workspaces to empower and lessen the feeling of loss of control.
- Communicate thoroughly, frequently, and honestly. To provide continuous updates and establish feedback systems to build unity and trust.
- Encourage daily check-ins between staff and administrators. To continually ask "Are you okay?" cannot be overstated and is especially important when working in a remote virtual environment. Over communicate this message.
- Be prepared to make special accommodations for employees who are either at high-risk or who perceive themselves to be at higher risk of COVID-19. complications. To be open to talking about and making accommodations.
- Create a more relaxed, fun atmosphere that encourages employees to laugh. To have fun.
- Focus on wellness. To promote health activities and create opportunities for faculty to get support.
- Encourage employees to take advantage of district-sponsored employee assistance program resources. To engage in developing an employee assistance program if not currently available.

(Velez, 2020, para. 12–18)

The Needs of Students. As schools transition back to school during fall 2020, regardless of the configuration, school leaders and teachers must address not only potential learning loss but also understand and address the emotional disruptions experienced by students. Students need to make sense of what happened so they can move forward. The sample self-reflection questions presented in Table 5.2 can support students in making sense of the context they find themselves.

Dr. Jill A. Baker, the superintendent of the Long Beach Unified School District (LBUSD), understood the gravity of COVID-19 from its onset, and in her Narrative she describes her district's journey to meet the needs

109

Supporting Social and Emotional Needs

Table 5.2 Self-reflection questions

Competency	Sample self-reflection questions
Self-awareness: Aaccurately recognize one's own emotions, thoughts, and values and how they influence behavior.	• How do I identify, recognize, and name my emotions in the moment? • How do I recognize the relationship between my feelings and my reactions to people and situations?
Self-management: Successfully regulate one's emotions, thoughts, and behaviors in different situations—effectively managing stress, controlling impulses, and motivating oneself.	• How do I manage my emotions and channel them in useful ways without harming anyone? • How do I stay calm, clear-headed, and unflappable under high stress and during a crisis?
Social awareness: Take the perspective of and empathize with others, including those from diverse backgrounds and cultures.	• How do I actively grasp another person's perspective and feelings from both verbal and nonverbal cues? • Do I generally believe people are doing their best, and do I expect the best of them?
Relationship skills: Establish and maintain healthy and rewarding relationships with diverse individuals and groups.	• How do I foster an emotionally nurturing and safe environment for staff, students, families, and community members? • How am I open and authentic with others about my values and beliefs, goals, and guiding principles?
Responsible decision-making: Make constructive choices about personal behavior and social interactions based on ethical standards, safety concerns, and social norms.	• How am I able to define the core of the problem and differentiate it from solution options? • How do I recognize the need for change, to challenge the status quo, and to encourage new thinking in my school?

Adapted from CASEL (n.d.c).

110

of their students. LBUSD is an urban system that serves 70,000 preK-12 students supported by 3,400 classroom teachers and more than 7,000 other certificated and classified staff. Dr. Baker has worked for 28 years at LBUSD as a successful teacher, principal, and central office administrator. Her leadership contributed to increased student achievement, the development of multiple district-wide initiatives and systems, and a culture of appreciation and continuous improvement. Dr. Baker's efforts have led her system to numerous national accolades as well as regional recognition by multiple agencies including being named the Education Champion by the Mayor's Fund for Education and the Secondary Education Award from the Long Beach Branch NAACP.

Dr. Baker led us through her journey and the lessons she and her system learned as they programmatically pivoted in meeting new and continuously emerging challenges as the pandemic swept her school district. Underlying every decision was keeping a laser focus on ensuring equity and maintaining continuity.

Jill A. Baker, Ed.D.
Superintendent of Schools
Long Beach Unified School District
Long Beach, CA

Lessons Learned While Navigating the Unknown

Doesn't every school district have a pandemic plan? Of course. But, how many of those districts ever thought that they would need to dig that plan out from the proverbial back shelf and actually use it? We didn't. Our pandemic plan was supposed to get us through a localized outbreak of something like the Norovirus or a bad flu year, both of which we have had to manage in the past. However, the events of 2020 have redefined our understanding of the terms "pandemic" and "unprecedented," and I am not sure that I will ever be able to utter those words again without flashing back to the days of 2020 and considering what this time has meant to the 70,000 students and 10,000 employees of the Long Beach Unified School District (LBUSD).

Supporting Social and Emotional Needs

Even when we closed our 85 schools on Friday, March 13, we had no idea what managing a pandemic would actually look like and feel like in our local context, and we certainly didn't know how long it would go on. The only thing that we knew for sure was that our first action needed to be to ensure that every student who relied on their school for breakfast or lunch had a place to go on Monday morning for a nutritious meal. We had one weekend to activate our pandemic plan and get to work, and that is exactly what we did. We served meals across the city every day until the school year finished. I wish I could say that the decisions that followed were made that easily.

Between 2016 and 2019, students across LBUSD had become more and more adept in the use of technology as we became a school district where each student had a tablet or laptop computer. Our youngest pre-school and kindergarten students regularly used programs like ST Math, our older elementary students made Google slides for classroom presentations, and our secondary students turned to technology to conduct classroom research, to turn in assignments and to collaborate with students across campus (or across the globe). Many of our teachers and leaders studied the Substitution, Augmentation, Modification and Redefinition (SAMR) model of technology integration and worked hard to redefine classroom learning and the related tasks through the use of technology (Puentedura, 2014). However, during the pandemic, our teachers had to both learn to teach from a distance, and adapt to "living" at a distance.

When our students and staff left their buildings to go home and shelter in place, the gravity of the situation was not clear. I remember wondering aloud if school might be out for more than a couple of weeks, then a month passed and then two and finally we had to face the reality that we wouldn't be able to bring students back to our buildings through the end of the school year.

Looking back, it wasn't the technology itself that posed the greatest challenge for us. We distributed 30,000 Chromebooks, and our first purchase after closing our buildings was for 5,000 hotspots. We did encounter a challenge getting the 5,000 hotspots into the hands of our families who needed them. But it was the challenge of recreating the connection, the inspiration, and the motivation that are triggered through contact between teachers and peers and peers to peers that presented the greatest difficulty. In fact, the combination of learning from an adult, while in the presence of

112

Supporting Social and Emotional Needs

other similar-aged peers is central to the "magic" that happens in a classroom and may have been underestimated until now.

Because the entire country experienced versions of the same pandemic, I will spare readers the retelling of the struggle and offer some of our team's insights that came as we led (and continue to lead) through this global health crisis. These are lessons that we are using ourselves as we enter another school year facing many of the same challenges that we did in the spring.

What Have We Learned About Leading in Hard Times?

- **Center students in our decision-making.** Centering students, especially those who will be more negatively impacted by a decision, requires adults to step back, consider their "why" and choose courage over comfort. Ask, "Which students benefit from this decision?" and "Which students may be harmed by this decision?"

- **Create systems now, not when a pandemic hits.** Systems require a leader, a simple or complex process, and people, all of which are critical during a pandemic and in good times. Systems that are recorded in writing allow anyone and everyone to be on the team that works together to address a challenge. Ask, "How am I documenting this system?"

- **Keep equity at the forefront.** During difficult times, it is natural to be so overwhelmed by the immediate that we forget about the work that we were doing before difficulty hit. Difficult times exacerbate inequities. We must keep our eyes on the future and ask, "Through the lens of equity, how should this problem be addressed?"

- **Conduct empathy interviews as part of our decision-making process.** If you are able, study the use of design thinking, which includes building empathy as a critical component of developing solutions or use simple tools, such as those found in the Californians for Justice (n.d.) publication, *6 Things that Teachers Can Do to Build Relationships with Students*, to stay focused on student needs. Listening and empathy allows each of us to stand alongside another human and hear about their lived experience. Ask, "What do I need to know about how you are experiencing the world?"

Supporting Social and Emotional Needs

- **Create a team and be a good team member.** Leaders need to be both, and both are required for work that sticks. But, it is easy for all of us to isolate, complete our tasks, and not lean into the difficulty of the time together. Ask, "How am I showing up for my team? Am I contributing to our collective success?"
- **Care for yourself.** Isn't it interesting how much self-care has emerged during the pandemic? In Fisher et al.'s (2020) recent publication, *The Distance Learning Playbook*, Module 1 is entitled "Take Care of Yourself." Ask, "If I don't take care of myself, who will?"

As I write this Narrative, it has been almost four and a half months of leading and navigating through a pandemic. We are preparing to reopen school in the Long Beach Unified School District, and we face many of the challenges that were present in March. Did I mention that my first interview for Superintendent of Schools was on March 16? I have transitioned from Deputy Superintendent of Schools to Superintendent of Schools and will never forget this time for the rest of my life. On my office wall is a beautiful image created by artist and illustrator Kadir Nelson (2020) entitled, *After the Storm*. It is an image of hope and humanity, and I look at it as often as possible because it reminds me that there will be renewed life and new possibilities after this storm.

Dr. Baker remained steadfast in her convictions and optimism in her system's future as she navigated changes and prepared for what would likely be a new normal for the students and teachers in her district. We can learn many lessons from the empathy of Dr. Jill Baker.

New Thinking Moving Forward

The emotional drain from essentially turning the education world upside-down has created significant emotional turbulence. The most asked question right now for students and teachers is: "When can we get back to normal?"

Supporting Social and Emotional Needs

Teachers, who have been this country's bedrock in supporting students, are now requiring more personal and professional support as they navigate through new virtual instructional models and develop relationships with their students. Students are seeing the picture of school as they knew it disappearing and asking *why* and *what do I do now?* While much focus has been on new instructional models, the social and emotional needs of teachers and students will also require new thinking to replace the traditional structures formally found in the schoolhouse.

Moving Forward

The social and emotional impact of the schoolhouse shutdown and movement to full virtual learning will not fully disappear. Moving into fall 2020, many school systems opted to start the year later and to begin virtually given the surge in COVID-19 cases. While schools across the country have responded to many crises in the past, this response was different. Lanoue (2020) explains, "Opening schools and meeting the diverse needs of all children post COVID-19 is likely the most daunting task ever undertaken by our nation's public schools" (para. 14). Much different than previous movements to solely improve academic performance, teachers and leaders are now called upon to create new paths in educating children and keeping them safe.

In this time of unknowns, the focus on the emotional needs of children must outweigh the academic focus. The transition(s) back to school will bring about many emotions from happiness to fear as students reconnect with their peers and teachers. Responding to these social and emotional needs when schools reopen and beyond will not be a one-time fix and requires new long-term support systems.

Webs of Support for Students. Teachers and leaders must ready themselves to systematically design a web of support to meet the emotional impact caused from the fears and isolation created from COVID-19. According to Teaching Tolerance (2020), the inability for students to be at their schools impacted their sense of safety and diminished feelings of connectedness and hope. As schools plan for students to start the new year, processes should be developed to:

Supporting Social and Emotional Needs

1. **Create a sense of safety:** Students' basic needs are important as community institutions are closed and families experience layoffs, loss of income, struggles to buy food and pay for housing.

2. **Reestablish connectedness:** Students feel the impact of being isolated due to community restrictions, social distancing, and the closing of public places important to socialize.

3. **Support hope:** Students feel a sense of hopelessness where they will not return to their normal lives filled with sports, the arts and all the social events that have traditionally been mainstreamed in education.

During disruptions, it is especially important to focus on safety through semblances of rituals and routines.

In virtual environments, establishing new routines of a daily schedule and understanding its impact on students has emerged as a priority to reduce anxiety in students. The Baltimore City Schools developed a framework to address students' psychosocial and emotional needs in virtual environments (Krueger, 2020):

1. **Check in with students on a regular basis:** Probably one of the simplest forms of connecting with students with the largest return to support their social and emotional needs.

2. **Establish a balance between structure and flexibility:** Students need to have a schedule to establish routines but due to varying home situations need the flexibility which requires synchronous and asynchronous learning activities.

3. **Create collaborative learning opportunities:** Learning is a social construct and students are social, requiring online opportunities to collaborate and connect personally.

4. **Understand and engage student sadness:** The loss of the anticipated activities and often "rites of passage" may no longer exist and students need to process this with knowing the challenges of COVID-19.

5. **Do more for students who are struggling:** The impact on students varies tremendously and some students just need more teacher support.

116

Supporting Social and Emotional Needs

As schools continue educating students from a distance, new systems were needed to support emerging social emotional needs.

Making shifts in existing programs to meet the new challenges brought on by COVID-19 became a top priority for Mr. Rich Merlo, superintendent of the Corcoran Joint Unified School District (CUSD) in Corcoran, California. CUSD serves 3,303 students supported by 189 classroom teachers and 70 classified staff members.

In his Narrative, Mr. Merlo shared not only his insights about what his system learned about the types of support students needed during the disruption caused by the COVID-19 pandemic, but he also shared how systems owned this type of work. Through inclusive processes across the district, Mr. Merlo observed system ownership of their solutions.

Mr. Rich Merlo
Superintendent
Corcoran Joint Unified School District
Corcoran, CA

We Really Did Own It

Who could have predicted we would end up owning a challenge that none of us could have ever dreamed of? Our theme for this school year has been "We Own It!" Ultimately, we ended up owning something much bigger than we expected.

When we discussed the theme for the 2019–2020 school year, we recognized the importance of our Personalized Learning Vision for the District:

> We will partner with our students to own their learning, pursue their ambitions, and achieve their goals.

The words "own their learning" stood out. When students take responsibility and own their learning, and we own our responsibility as professionals to make sure every student learns and grows in their education, we have achieved what we set out to do. That is, we have created lifelong learners who will achieve and succeed in life.

With the pandemic that forced our kids and staff to their homes to continue school, all of us did not have a choice. We had to own the challenges

Supporting Social and Emotional Needs

that come with a forced distance learning environment. What was so encouraging for our schools and community was that our staff and students were ready for the challenge. We already owned the challenge to make sure every child in our district had access to the technology needed to learn anywhere in the world, let alone in their own home in that:

- almost 100% of our students across K-12 have had a state-of-the art device at home with Internet access;
- a vast majority of our staff were trained to use technology that personalizes and leverages student learning;
- a vast majority of our staff were trained to use technology for learning for all students in dynamic and different ways;
- many of our staff members relentlessly kept track of our kids and made sure they were caught up in their learning;
- many staff members were diligent in reaching out to students who have social emotional needs throughout distancing.

However, to meet the challenges, we had to bring focus to our priorities, mission, vision, values, and goals. We did so first by communicating with all staff and instructing them on our focus with our Distance Learning Program.

We knew that interpersonal communication was going to be a huge challenge. The emphasis had to be placed on continuing and building relationships and student emotional, mental, and spiritual well-being. We then worked with our teachers to adopt and to build Distance Learning Correlates in our work to educate kids without direct contact.

Distance Learning Correlates
We provide the best learning environment in the world by relentlessly collaborating, sharing effective strategies, and supporting best practices!

- We have resolved to make personal connections with every student to learn and grow with high standards.
- We are all part of a great team that is more prepared for this than ever!
- We are committed to continue to build and nurture our relationships with our students.

Supporting Social and Emotional Needs

- We emphasize quality of instruction over quantity of work; we go deeper with fewer standards.
- We expect students to be challenged and receive timely feedback.
- We pursue and reach out to every failing or missing student through and beyond facility closures.
- We celebrate and share teacher and student victories.

Personal connection is the number one ingredient to growth in unprecedented times. Virtually or in-class, it is about the teacher who changes students' lives to help them reach their destiny.

Here's What We Saw and Learned

We made it a priority to archive and celebrate many of the victories and successes we had with our students and staff. We saw the teachers of special needs students making "safe" home visits. We learned that many of our students had to have some type of face-to-face contact. Our staff became more dogged in "not letting kids off the hook," and they worked together with our psychologists, mental health technical staff, and counselors to create and follow through on credible referrals for kids who showed signs of despair and even behavior indicating potential self-harm.

Counselors followed suit and experienced many small victories with students who just needed that extra touch, albeit through a screen. There is the story of our middle school office staff who reached out to a family stricken by COVID-19 and rallied other staff members to provide care packages. We had many successes about how teachers stepped up in their lesson planning and execution to meet student needs among many others. These are a small sample of the many successes we experienced through outreach beyond a digital device that demonstrated the heart and mindset that came from a staff focused on the right thing—students and their families.

In my blog describing the theme for this school year, our system was prophetic in how we explained how we "owned" this crisis:

> We see the ownership that takes responsibility for the good, the bad and the indifferent and refuses to blame others. We own the failures and reject excuses and faultfinding. Problems are owned to be solved, and solutions are owned by all and shared to implement, succeed, and celebrate!

> (Merlo, 2019, para. 6)

Supporting Social and Emotional Needs

Looking back, we are proud of students and staff for taking owner-ship of the solution of doing everything possible to make sure our kids are safe and still learn, albeit from a distance. We witnessed teachers, administrators and classified staff members who stepped up and "filled holes" that had to be filled. As a district leader, I could not be more satisfied to see how so many staff members took leadership roles almost spontan-eously in response to adversity. In many ways, our work was motivated and formed to bring to life the words of Brené Brown who said, "If you own this story, you get to write the ending."

This coming year will be one where we emphasize and promote our ability to "own our story" and thereby create the road and destiny built on our mission, vision, values, and lofty goals. When we own it, we call the shots and help everyone finish strong!

Mr. Merlo recognized and articulated the core principles that were already at the foundation of their district which helped them in meeting the social and emotional needs of their students while maintaining a challen-ging academic program.

Webs of Support for Teachers. The COVID-19 pandemic created a focus long overdue—the well-being of teachers. Teachers and leaders are now having to engage in the challenges of child safety not only in their schools, but also in their families as well. As schools move forward, meeting the social and emotional needs of teachers must be more compre-hensive. Teachers are now expressing concerns about their safety and the safety of their colleagues. As schools reopen, it is expected that 20% of the teaching force will not return to their profession while others will not be able or refuse to return to the physical classroom.

When the school doors closed and routines changed, the reaction was a high level of panic because teachers could not fulfill their responsibilities. According to a survey by Teaching for Tolerance (Collins, 2020), teachers indicated they needed:

1. Recommendations for online resources.

2. Emotional support.

Supporting Social and Emotional Needs

3. Materials that intersected COVID-19 and social justice.
4. Best practices for distance learning.
5. Physical and printable resources for students not online.
6. Resources to support parents in their role as teachers.

While teachers were faced with their own safety issues, they continued to focus on fulfilling their responsibilities as teachers.

Making the Shift. Teaching in virtual spaces starts with a mind shift, and Merrill (2020) offered that teachers should:

1. **Expect trial and plenty of error:** Be reasonable with yourself in what you are trying to accomplish and be a peace with it.
2. **Acknowledge the extraordinary:** Reset your baseline while operating in the shadow of a global pandemic because it is not business as usual.
3. **Reduce the workload for yourself and others:** Do less if possible to attend to your own life and family needing added care.
4. **Look for ways to reduce isolation:** No person is an island. Working in a shelter-in-place space can be depressing for both teachers and students.
5. **Remain optimistic:** Everyone thinks they can't before they can.
6. **Mind the gap:** The work will be hard, but there are students facing more severe challenges, and they need your support.

The COVID-19 environment created many mixed emotions for teachers, facing the new challenges of teaching their students without being with them in person, balancing life with their own children, and navigating the many emotions of trying to do it all—in isolation without support. Teachers need to examine their emotions and create coping strategies to move forward and school leaders must support these efforts (see Chapter 7, "Leading Through the Unknown"). Table 5.3 describes teachers' feelings, their causes, and how teachers can cope with these emerging emotions post-COVID-19.

Much of the focus for schools in moving forward has been on understanding the world as students see it, and the role of the adults in providing them with guidance and support. As this pandemic

Supporting Social and Emotional Needs

Table 5.3 Coping with emotions—post-COVID-19

Feelings	Causes	Coping
Anxious Overwhelmed	Fear of COVID-19 and taking the necessary precautions	1. Remain positive, see successes 2. Stay connected with family 3. Take time to engage in hobbies or personal activities
Lonely Sad Irritable	Isolation from friends, family, and coworkers	1. Make connections online 2. Explore self-interests 3. Think positively about what you want in the future
Stress Frustration Anger	Uncertainty of tomorrow and getting back to the way it was	1. Live for the day and enjoy 2. Others are experiencing the same isolations 3. You are not alone
Bored Lethargic	Lack of structure and routines	1. Create routines 2. Keep a schedule 3. Maintain regular "normal" routines

Adapted from Cipriano and Brackett (2020) and Rethink (2020).

unfolds, supporting teachers in fulfilling their responsibilities must be recognized and acted upon by school leaders. In this new environment, maintaining the health of the adults is as important as the focus on the health of students.

Leading for Tomorrow

Schools play a critical role in the socialization of students and interwoven into this role is the responsibility to support students and their social emotional needs along the way. With COVID-19, the role of schools meeting the social emotional needs of students grew and new challenges emerged on how to support school personnel as they fulfilled their responsibilities. Schools responded by:

- implementing new processes and structures to support the social needs of students in the virtual environment;

- developing formal programs in response to the impact of COVID-19 on students' social, emotional, and cognitive growth;

- creating stability and balance in addressing the academic and social needs of students whether in a virtual or in school environment;

- understanding and responding to the personal and professional emotional stress of teachers who are on the front-lines with students every day.

The school's role in addressing the social emotional needs of students intensified by the impact of the schoolhouse shutdown and a growing need emerged to address the social emotional needs of their faculty and staff as they fulfilled their responsibilities.

References

Alliance for Excellent Education. (2018). Did you know? Adolescents are… *Alliance for Excellent Education.* https://mk0all4edorgjxiy8xf9.kinstacdn.com/wp-content/uploads/2018/12/SAL-SEL-Infographic.pdf

Brown, B. (n.d.). Quotable quotes. *Goodreads.* www.goodreads.com/quotes/641983-if-you-own-this-story-you-get-to-write-the

Californians for Justice. (n.d). 6 things teachers can do to build relationships with students. *Californians for Justice.* https://caljustice.org/

CASEL. (n.d.a). What is SEL? *CASEL.* https://casel.org/what-is-sel/

CASEL. (n.d.b). Core SEL competencies. *CASEL.* https://casel.org/core-competencies/

CASEL. (n.d.c). Adult SEL self-assessment. *CASEL.* https://schoolguide.casel.org/resource/adult-sel-self-assessment/

Cipriano, C., & Brackett, M. (2020, April 7). Teachers are anxious and overwhelmed. They need SEL now more than ever. *EdSurge.* www.edsurge.com/news/2020-04-07-teachers-are-anxious-and-overwhelmed-they-need-sel-now-more-than-ever

Collins, C. (2020, March 19). Teaching through coronavirus: What educators need right now. *Teaching Tolerance.* www.tolerance.org/magazine/teaching-through-coronavirus-what-educators-need-right-now

Cristóvão, A. M., Candeias, A. A., & Verdasca, J. (2017). Social and emotional learning and academic achievement in Portuguese schools: A bibliometric study. *Frontiers in Psychology, 8,* 1913. https://doi.org/10.3389/fpsyg.2017.01913

Dewey, J. (1897). My pedagogic creed. *The School Journal, 54*(3), 77–80.

Durlak, J. A., & Mahoney, J. L. (2019, December). The practical benefits of an SEL program. *CASEL.* https://casel.org/wp-content/uploads/2019/12/Practical-Benefits-of-SEL-Program.pdf

Fisher, D., Frey, N., & Hattie, J. (2020). *The distance learning playbook: Teaching for engagement and impact in any setting.* Corwin Press.

Garcia, A., & Mirra, N. (2020, June 17). Teachers need opportunities to heal before the school year begins. *EdSource.* https://edsource.org/2020/teachers-need-opportunities-to-heal-before-the-school-year-begins/633287?fbclid=IwAR3SK5eT6W-tY8IMpDneHeTONShRr5SBXkFPaI_vSUWeZzk_OyM2afrEuto

Jones, S., Brush, K., Bailey, R., Brion-Meisels, G., McIntyre, J., Kahn, J., & Stickle, L. (2017). Navigating SEL from the inside out: Looking inside & across 25 leading SEL programs: A practical resource for schools and OST providers (Elementary School Focus). *The Wallace Foundation.* www.wallacefoundation.org/knowledge-center/Documents/Navigating-Social-and-Emotional-Learning-from-the-Inside-Out.pdf

Krueger, N. (2020, April 7). Meeting students' social-emotional needs during a COVID-19 lockdown. *ISTE.* www.iste.org/explore/meeting-students-social-emotional-needs-during-covid-19-lockdown

Lanoue, P. D. (2020). Schools are the epicenter of a community. *Facilitron.* www.facilitron.com/resources/news/schools-are-the-epicenter-of-a-community-phil-lanoue/

Mahoney, J. L., Durlak, J. A., & Weissberg, R. P. (2018). An update on social and emotional learning outcome research. *Phi Delta Kappan, 100*(4), 18–23. https://doi.org/10.1177/0031721718881568

Massachusetts Department of Elementary and Secondary Education. (n.d.). Multi-tiered system of support. *Massachusetts Department of*

Elementary and Secondary Education. www.doe.mass.edu/sfss/mtss/blueprint.pdf

Medway Public Schools. (2019). Strategic plan: Excellence for All 2019–2024. *Medway Public Schools*. https://medwayschools.org/UserFiles/Servers/Server_547022/File/School%20Committee/Presentations/Strategic%20Plan%2019%202024.pdf

Merlo, R. (2019, August 2). We own it! *Rich Merlo* https://richmerlo.blogspot.com/2019/08/we-own-it.html

Merrill, S. (2020, March 19). Teaching through a pandemic: A mindset for this moment. *Edutopia*. www.edutopia.org/article/teaching-through-pandemic-mindset-moment?gclid=EAIaIQobChMIlJGA6L-f6gIViK_ICh31PA_TEAMYASAAEgLhe_D_BwE

Moffitt, T. E., Arseneault, L., Belsky, D., Dickson, N., Hancox, R. J., Harrington, H., Houts, R., Poulton, R., Roberts, B. W., Ross, S., Sears, M. R., Thomson, W. M., & Caspi, A. (2011). A gradient of childhood self-control predicts health, wealth, and public safety. *Proceedings of the National Academy of Sciences, 108*(7), 2693–2698. https://doi.org/10.1073/pnas.1010076108

National Association of School Psychologists. (n.d.). Social skills: Promoting positive behavior, academic success, and school safety. *NASP*. www.naspcenter.org/factsheets/socialskills_fs.html

National Education Association. (2018). The importance of social emotional learning for all students across all grades. *Backgrounder*. www.nea.org/assets/docs/Social%20and%20Emotional%20Learning%20Response_Bkgdr%20v3.pdf

Nelson, K. (2020, April 10). After the storm. *Kadie Nelson*. www.kadirnelson.com

Page, S. (2020, May 27). Back to school? 1 in 5 teachers are unlikely to return to reopened classrooms this fall, poll says. *USA Today*. www.usatoday.com/story/news/education/2020/05/26/coronavirus-schools-teachers-poll-ipsos-parents-fall-online/5254729002/

Puentedura, R.R. (2014, December 9). SAMR and the EdTech Quintet: Designing learning, designing for assessment. *Hippasus*. www.hippasus.com/rrpweblog/archives/2014_12.html

Supporting Social and Emotional Needs

Responsive Classroom. (June 7, 2016). What is a morning meeting? *Responsive Classroom.* www.responsiveclassroom.org/what-is-morning-meeting/

Rethink. (2020). Supporting youth, teachers and families worldwide through the COVID-19 pandemic. *Rethink.* www.rethinkstigma.org/covid-19-support.html

SCAN. (n.d.). Social development in children. *SCAN.* www.scanva.org/support-for-parents/parent-resource-center-2/social-development-in-children/

Teaching Tolerance. (2020, March 23). A trauma-informed approach to teaching through coronavirus. *Teaching Tolerance.* www.tolerance.org/magazine/a-trauma-informed-approach-to-teaching-through-coronavirus

Velez, A. (2020, May 6). Fostering safety and confidence as employees return to schools. *District Administration.* https://districtadministration.com/fostering-safety-and-confidence-as-employees-return-to-schools/?eml=20200513&oly_enc_id=6799J8347367J8A

Wiglesworth, M., Lendrum, A., Oldfield, J., Scott, A., ten Bokkel, I., Tate, K., & Emery, C. (2016). The impact of trial stage, developer involvement and international transferability on universal social and emotional learning programme outcomes: A meta-analysis. *Cambridge Journal of Education, 46*(3), 347–376. https://doi.org/10.1080/0305764X.2016.1195791

6 | The Roles of Schools and Their Communities

In This Chapter...

Introduction	127
Community Relationships	128
Narrative: *Leveraging Local Leadership During a Global Crisis*	130
Schools and Healthy Children	135
Narrative: *Communities Respond in Uncharted Territory*	137
Student Well-being in a Virtual Environment	142
Narrative: *Leading for Wellness When All is Not Well: Lessons from COVID-19*	143
Leading for Tomorrow	147
References	147

Introduction

The COVID-19 pandemic brought forward a strong message that communities needed to respond to the well-being and health needs of students, teachers, and their families as "one." The relationships between community agencies, including the local government and the business sector with schools, are typically defined by their history within the community and leaders' efforts to create and sustain these relationships. With the COVID-19 pandemic, systematic revelations emerged about the broad work of schools that permeated almost every aspect of their communities. Ensuring the safety of its students and teachers became a part of a larger picture that illustrates how changes in the routines of schools impacted their communities.

The multiple roles of schools and their importance to the fabric of a community became more apparent as schools shut their doors. The first response within hours was to ensure students would not go hungry by putting into action complex plans to provide breakfast and lunch for students using creative delivery methods. In the following days, schools responded to the growing need to access services typically coordinated through schools. This chapter explores new relationships necessary for schools and their communities collectively to support the growth and development of the children in their communities.

 ## Community Relationships

As a result of the pandemic, schools cannot reopen in isolation. Important for educational leaders, regardless of political history, is to work alongside all community organizations, in tandem, to safely reopen the schoolhouse doors. Communities must come together as one. The new reality with COVID-19 is rethinking the collective work between school districts with local government, business, and community agencies so that each can function together in response to disruptions related to health or other community-wide issues such as pandemics, racial incidents, etc.

Emerging Community Roles

The role of schools in providing services outside the central functions of teaching and learning is not new. Nutrition, dental care, health care, substance abuse, and child abuse are just a sampling of how schools serve in their communities. Now, the school's role in supporting their communities other than education is being highlighted by the complexities brought forth during this pandemic.

Models of school and community hubs are not new and traditionally have been formed around national challenges such as poverty, school

Roles of Schools and Their Communities

performance, or health care. Existing models of community hubs were typically designed to support the academic success of its students. According to Horn et al.:

> When a school integrates and begins to function as a hub, it organizes services for its own students as well as, in certain cases, the broader school community such as parents and other family members in an effort to improve the chances for students to excel academically.
>
> (Horn et al., 2015, p. 4)

Now, the concept of community hubs creates an expanded focus to the health and welfare of not only students but also for the greater community served by the school and the district. A new question for schools and communities as they move forward will be "How do we define our individual and collective roles in addressing community needs in the COVID-19 pandemic?"

While the focus for schools should primarily be about how to educate the children, they now have an increasing role in the health of students and adults in their community. For schools to open their doors, they will need to work directly with community agencies in developing plans that will likely redefine relationships and allocation of resources. Decisions on school reopening models and response to student needs must be made with coordinated planning between the school system, local government, and the business community.

Dr. Calvin J. Watts, superintendent of the Kent School District (Kent, Washington), emphatically and equitably embraces the power of the people in his district and community. The Kent School District serves 27,000 students supported by 3,600 employees, including 1,600 classroom teachers and 2,000 school-based and central office staff. Dr. Watts began his 28-year career in education as a teacher in the Seattle Public Schools. Dr. Watts spent 13 years in Gwinnett County Public Schools (GA), where he engaged diverse communities and improved student performance as a building and central office-level administrator. As superintendent of the Kent School District, Dr. Watts implemented a bold, new entry plan that inspired the development of the community-based strategic planning process that drives continuous quality improvement district-wide. He increased student access to more challenging high school course offerings and the district showed significant gains across special education, Black/

Roles of Schools and Their Communities

African American and Hispanic/Latino subgroups Kent School District's Class of 2019 recorded the all-time highest four-year adjusted cohort graduation rate of 84%.

There was no time to wait in addressing the unknowns of COVID-19 and its impact on Dr. Watts's district and community. He understood the need to respond immediately through continuous communication with all stakeholders. Through his Narrative, Dr. Watts amplified the urgency to address the educational injustices within the system as he engaged diverse communities in larger discussions in leading the system.

Calvin J. Watts, Ed.D.
Superintendent
Kent School District
Kent, WA

Leveraging Local Leadership During a Global Crisis

A leader whom I admire greatly often stated, "If you believe that public education is devoid of politics, then you also believe that you can swim without getting wet." Throughout my 28 years in education, I have also come to realize that politics can best be described as the relationship between power and people. As a result, whether a Fortune 500 company, a startup nonprofit organization, a faith-based institution, or even the family's place of residence, a high-functioning entity can be characterized by the ability of its people to share and shift that power empathetically and equitably. When the opposite occurs—when power is instead hoarded or abused—then the outcomes can be harmful to an individual and to an entire community.

Health and Well-being of the Community, First
Since 2015, I have proudly served as the Superintendent of the Kent School District, the fifth largest and fourth most richly diverse school system in Washington State. During the months of January and February 2020, the Pacific Northwest became known as the epicenter for COVID-19 positive cases. Through initial pandemic planning, our school community soon realized that these health-related circumstances were devastating and, if left up to chance, the impact could place 27,000 students, 3,600

employees, and 19,000 families in harm's way. In fact, our first critical decision concerning the health and well-being of our community occurred on February 28, 2020. After basing our decision on a preponderance of evidence, and consulting with district staff and local public health officials, I recommended that we close two schools for deep cleaning and disinfecting on March 2–3, 2020.

The concerns expressed by families, students, and staff were impossible to ignore. So we continued to communicate early and often about the possibility of community spread and the importance of preventative care, including washing hands, social distancing, and staying home when you are not feeling well. We also communicated through several mediums that we closed those school facilities out of an abundance of caution and based on information that was shared with district officials.

Appreciation for the Voices of the Community

The importance of maintaining a safe and healthy environment was our primary concern. It was not until we reopened that I gained a full appreciation for the overall concerns expressed by our community. The fears associated with contracting the COVID-19 virus were prominently displayed when we opened both schools on March 4, 2020. It was important for me to be the face of care and compassion, so I personally welcomed our families, students, and staff back to their respective school communities. I praised our staff for their commitment to teaching and learning, and for their focus on the safety, health, and well-being of our students. I also thanked our families for trusting us to take good care of their most precious resource, their children. In fact, these two school facilities were now the cleanest and most disinfected facilities within our entire school building portfolio. Ironically, for the next two weeks, both schools registered the lowest student attendance rates for the year.

Together Creating Comfort and Strength

By this time, our communication strategies had become more pronounced and included the voices of health practitioners, educational service district staff, as well as locally elected and appointed leaders in the community, including our Mayors, Chamber of Commerce President, State Superintendent, School Board Directors, and local Superintendent colleagues. It was clear to each one of us that the problem we were

Roles of Schools and Their Communities

attempting to solve, presented neither simple nor easy solutions. We found both comfort and strength in numbers. Even in the midst of this emerging crisis, my superintendent colleagues and I took solace in the fact that we were all going through this global health crisis together. As a result of this emerging leadership challenge, our regional education service district scheduled semiweekly meetings to ensure a consistency of purpose, practice, and information-sharing was available to all school districts. More often than not, we were able to have thought-provoking and safe conversations that enabled us to voice concerns, frustrations, and even fears about what no educator wants to consider—the inability to adequately address the varied needs of our students, staff, and families we serve.

Working as One

On March 16, 2020, we discovered just how impactful public education had become to so many. As a result of our Governor's Executive Order, and our State Superintendent's "First Do No Harm" guidance, each of our state's 295 school districts were required to provide breakfast and lunch meal service to students, free childcare for essential workers, and to maintain the delivery of instruction within a remote learning environment. Over the next five months, we worked collectively with our labor partners, local community-based organizations (CBOs), faith-based institutions, and private businesses associated with our Kent Chamber of Commerce, to address the most basic needs of our students, families, and staff members.

Between the months of March and June 2020, the Kent School District along with several community-based partners:

- served more than 650,000 meals;
- provided digital devices and Wi-Fi hotspots to more than 7,000 students and families who had not already been supported by our Digital 1:1 Program; and,
- provided free childcare to more than 50 families who were considered essential workers.

In these unprecedented times, our local government, school districts, and CBOs exemplified what we have all come to recognize about the

132

Roles of Schools and Their Communities

power of local leadership within a global health crisis—it is not measured in what happens, it can only be measured in how we respond to the individual needs of a person, a family, an organization, or an entire community.

Educational Justice

An effective democratic republic is one that is informed, engaged, and empowered. If school systems like the Kent School District are to be recognized as public institutions that uphold and support the values of diversity, equity, and inclusion, then we must create the very systems, structures, and policies that will move us further toward educational justice.

Whether based on race, ethnicity, linguistic ability, or socioeconomic status, we have learned from our current COVID-19 health crisis that our existing systems are disproportionately benefitting and burdening students and families at even greater levels. For these reasons, the phrase "Think globally and act locally" has gained particular significance. The COVID-19 pandemic did more than create a pandemic response. It shined an intense light on what existed in our schools and communities already: we have an equity gap and we must act upon it.

Together We Can

I recognize, now more than ever, that our mission of successfully preparing all students for their futures will only be realized when our entire community feels included, engaged, empowered, and supported. We have shifted our focus to creating a culture of collective efficacy and collective impact. The implementation of diverse cross-functional advisories, committees, task forces, and action learning teams, has enabled team members to listen more effectively and learn from and with students, families, teachers, building administrators, local businesses, institutions of higher education, elected officials, and affinity networks that may be linked to topics pertinent to the overall success of the Kent School District. By implementing this comprehensive strategy, our school district community has strengthened its willingness and ability to be highly communicative and responsive to the needs of all of our communities that make us the Kent School District.

Roles of Schools and Their Communities

Broader Role of School Leaders

The struggles of our district and community have been unprecedented, but the realization of the role of schools in my community has emerged clearly. I, as superintendent, now embrace a greater responsibility to impact our schools and community through engagement and community inclusion. Today, I lead, serve, and support our entire community through active engagement at every level from the classroom to the statehouse.

This pandemic has also tested leaders across the country in ways never experienced in our history. It not only raised the threshold for safety in uncharted waters, but leveraged the need to act in creating more equitable schools and communities. I believe strongly that the success of our responses will be directly dependent on the collective responsibility and actions we take as leaders in leveraging new ideas and solutions. Ultimately, school leaders will need to reflect on their roles and responsibilities and make the changes necessary to support every student, every family member, and every community member. For me, this reflection began on March 2, 2020.

Dr. Watts shared how community collaboration was needed to address the COVID-19 challenges and how this work surfaced the educational injustices that needed greater focus and attention in the system. He worked closely within his community as decisions were made to ensure the health and safety of all its members.

For the first time, many communities will need to consider the unknowns of COVID-19 as they develop short-term entry plans together. Decisions made in isolation can likely create conflict, frustration, and a feeling of being minimized by some groups. As communities come together in developing joint plans, Reid (2020) suggests that city managers consider these common best practices:

1. **Plan for the proper oversight:** Communities need to have an oversight plan to coordinate both internal and external stakeholders.

2. **Know your community culture:** A community's culture is critical and coordination and compromise are critical as plans are developed

to reopen including government, businesses, service agencies, and schools.

3. **Organize resources for the reopening effort:** Reopening a community will require additional or reallocation of resources especially personnel as new safety protocols are put in place.

4. **Protect employees and citizens:** The single most critical issue in the COVID-19 response is the protection of employees and citizens while preserving the commonly held expectations of the community.

5. **Sanitize to reopen:** Every community organization will need to put in place new protocols for keeping their environment clean and safe, of which many may remain in place post-COVID-19.

6. **Communicate and collaborate on reopening plans:** Reopening will require tremendous coordination and agreement between workplaces, childcare, and schools to assure the pragmatic and safe reopening of communities.

These practices provide a structure of response that is readily applicable for any entity to respond to COVID-19 or similar disruptions.

New problems create new questions with unknown answers that require new thinking. In moving forward, schools and community agencies must come together in new ways to address emerging school and community health challenges like COVID-19.

Schools and Healthy Children

Although the responsibility for providing or coordinating health care for students is not new for schools, their role varies widely across the country. Some districts have pioneered implementing full service health clinic facilities in their schools while others have created strong partnerships with health providers within their communities. Others have made decisions to narrow their responsibilities for a range of reasons including the availability and access of health resources in their community or the lack of community resources.

School Clinics and Health Care Partnerships

This pandemic exposed weaknesses in schools and communities related to the health care required by students. With the impact of COVID-19, schools and community health care systems could no longer work independently. While schools and health care providers have attempted to provide quality care for students and families, widespread efforts are often stalled due to barriers associated with organizational policies, competing, or shortages in resources.

Price (2016) asserts that "When the education system is enlisted as a meaningful partner in the implementation of community-wide efforts to promote healthy development, they facilitate the delivery of accessible, effective, and integrated prevention and intervention support to students who need them most" (p. 14). Whether physical health or mental health and counseling services, schools cannot shoulder this responsibility alone. They need the help and support of community agencies that can engage with students, their parents and guardians, and the schools. School districts that assume an active role in the health of their students understand that "educating children is likely the biggest challenge to public education, and the most complex, with multiple moving parts in their community" (Lanoue & Zepeda, 2018, p. 38).

Dr. Nardos King, in her role as the Region 3 Assistant Superintendent of the Fairfax County Public Schools (FCPS), realized that school leaders needed to apply what they were learning during the pandemic. Fairfax County Public Schools located in Falls Church, Virginia is the tenth largest district in the U.S., educating 187,474 students supported by 12,488 classroom teachers and 12,412 staff who serve in one of the 198 schools that span five regions. Dr. King spent three years with Baltimore County Public Schools as an Assistant Superintendent of High Schools and Executive Director of Secondary Schools. She currently serves as the President-Elect of the National Alliance of Black School Educators.

The speed at which schools needed to respond when shutting their doors signaled the need for help: they needed their communities. Dr. King described this journey when she walked out of her office on the day the Fairfax County Public Schools closed their doors.

Nardos E. King Ed.D.
Assistant Superintendent, Region 3
Fairfax County Public Schools
Falls Church, VA

Communities Respond in Uncharted Territory

As I write this in August 2020, I have not been to my office since March 13, 2020. I remember the day like it was yesterday. When I walked out of the door that evening, I did not pack up most of my things. I did not think about my plants. I just backed up my laptop like I did every other day and walked out the door.

Our Superintendent closed our schools; however, when he made the decision, we did not know that the Governor of Virginia would follow him and close schools across the state for the next two weeks. The Governor stated that it would allow for schools to be deeply cleaned and that it would help slow the spread of the virus. On March 23, 220 Virginians were COVID-19 positive, and six people had died. The Governor closed our schools for the remainder of the 2019–2020 school year.

Shifting into Action to Serve Students

Our most immediate concern when we closed schools was to figure out a way that we could feed our students. Thirty-one percent of the students in Fairfax County Public Schools qualified for free or reduced meals. My region office worked closely with our Food and Nutrition Department to make sure we could open Grab and Go services to accommodate as many areas as possible in our region of 45 schools. It is amazing what they were able to accomplish over the last five months, coordinating and distributing over two million meals and counting.

The second most immediate concerns were setting up the distribution of laptops to students who did not have access to a device for distant learning. At that time, we were on a stay-home order; but since the schools were on the Governor's list of essential places people could travel to and from home, we knew we had work to do to get the devices in the hands of our students. Our principals and technology specialists worked with our central office teams to put safe processes in place,

Roles of Schools and Their Communities

and we made it happen. In a span of three weeks, we provided devices to students in grades 3–8 in a safe manner. It was stressful and time-consuming, and I was so proud of our school teams. We also worked with cable and Internet services to get hotspots in the homes of families who did not have access to the Internet.

For the first three weeks after we closed, we did not offer formal face-to-face learning to our students. We used that time to connect with as many families as possible and to prepare for the launch of our distant learning plan. We provided online resources and used our TV channels to provide learning opportunities. We were entering uncharted territory and creating a plan for learning and instruction in a way that had not been done before. Blended learning has been encouraged over the last few years, but many of our teachers have never had to teach online. It was a shift the county had to make with 14,400 teachers. After two weeks of training and preparation, laptop and MiFi distributions, meal distributions, and meetings every day, it was time to launch our distant learning plan.

Through this time, we worked with many community agencies, churches, and nonprofits to support our most vulnerable students and their families. We had to ensure that while working with these groups of community supporters, that processes were put in place to ensure the safety of both our staff and our families. Again, it was amazing to see that the groups who partnered with us during the year, did not skip a beat when it came to supporting our schools.

What We Learned

We learned a lot from our experience in the spring. We now know how to set up safe and efficient laptop and food distribution centers at our schools. We learned that many of our families do not have access to the Internet. Some even drove to schools and parked in the parking lots to connect to the Internet so their kids could participate in distance learning. We learned that we have greater inequities in our schools that must be addressed as we prepare for the opening of schools for the new school year. We learned that our leaders are committed, and our teachers are amazing. We learned that we must prepare and learn from our mistakes and do better for our students. Above all else, we learned that our students are counting on us.

Roles of Schools and Their Communities

Connecting What We Learned

- Communication was the key while we built our plan. We spent the summer preparing for the opening of this school year. We created task forces that included all stakeholder groups to ensure all voices were at the table. We had work groups that met many times a week to bring details to the plans.
- Feedback was essential. Getting constant feedback to ensure we were not missing anything was essential—out students count on us.
- Working with our county government and the health department was important to ensure that we were making the right decisions as scenarios changed.

Moving forward, it is our hope that we can pivot to a return to face-to-face instruction. To do this, we must work with stakeholder groups to create metrics that make sense before we make the shift back to brick and mortar experiences. Something that we desperately must recognize is that safety above all else must be at the front of our decision-making, and that is why our system will begin the fall 2020 school year virtually for the first six weeks.

What's Next

Before this pandemic, our schools were prepared for what to do in case of a fire, tornado, or active shooter. We are better prepared now on what to do in the case of a pandemic. We must also be prepared to shift to a virtual or face-to-face experience at a moment's notice. We must ensure that our professional development includes both face-to-face and online learning instruction. We must use synchronous and asynchronous learning.

Because we are learning how to keep instruction going when we must close schools for any reason, no longer will we need to stop learning when we have snow days or other interruptions to attendance. We understand that it is important that every student has access to a device.

Never again can we be caught off guard. We must have policies, procedures, and written plans in place to respond anytime we must close schools. We lost a lot of learning time in the spring of 2020. We must work hard to ensure we make up for that lost learning, especially for our students who qualify for special education and English language learner services.

Districts and schools cannot do this work alone. We must work with colleges and universities to ensure the curriculum includes blended learning standards. When disaster strikes, we must bring the right voices around the table, and consistent and clear communication is important. Most importantly, when a pandemic or other type of disruption occurs, we must grant grace to all.

Dr. King's journey highlighted the importance of schools and communities *acting together*. The health and welfare of students was foundational to social development and remained one of the primary responsibilities for both schools and communities.

Mental Health Support

The impact of schools shutting down and moving to fully online formats created increased social and emotional stress on students. Students lost contact with their peers. Graduation, proms, and other ceremonies that typically mark the end of the year and the movement to the next were cancelled. Students and teachers were not able to come to closure in the year they began together. In many school districts, the call for mental health support during the COVID-19 pandemic became even a greater priority than academic programs. Whether in a virtual setting or when returning to schools, students needed to acclimate to their new routines that may necessitate immediate and long-term interventions.

The stress for students, parents, teachers, and community groups did not abate during the summer as systems grappled with the many unknowns associated with COVID-19.

- What would school look like in the fall?
- Will parents have the choice in sending their children to school or keeping them at home?
- Will students, teachers, and other support staff feel safe returning to school?

These questions with no experience to draw from, ongoing contradictory reports about the spread of COVID-19, and political bantering about the economy became extremely stressful and complicated decision-making.

Prior to the outbreak of COVID-19, mental health services were provided to over 50% of the student population; however, Golberstein et al. (2020) reported that students did not receive the needed support during school shutdowns. Regardless of when students return to the schoolhouse, they will require deliberate attention to determine the assistance needed. Parents are very concerned about the emotional needs of their children. Calderon (2020) reported data from a Gallup Panel in which 43% parents indicated their children were already or close to experiencing social and emotional harm from social distancing. Earlier data from a Gallup Panel (Brenan, 2020) illustrated that parents—about 15%—were beginning to suffer from social distancing and the stress of their children being isolated.

Addressing these concerns as well as the already existing mental health issues will need attention for both the immediate and long-term. Asking critical questions in preparing to open schools helps to ensure students receive the support needed. Suggested questions from the Kentucky Department of Education include:

- What do we have in place to support students and staff who appear to be deeply sad, withdrawn, or in distress?
- What community resources do we have to support staff and students?
- Are our counselors situated to handle many individual counseling sessions with students in need?
- What do we have in place to support Tier 3 students (students who we think may be at risk of harming themselves or someone else)?
- Have we made time for our counselors to address the mental health of students through Tier 1 instruction (whole group guidance) and Tier 2 direct student services (individual or small group counseling)?
- Have we been clear on the protocol for teachers to let counselors know when a student is in distress and how they should go about doing this?
- What other support staff do we have in place to help students who need extra support?
- What buddy/peer support systems can be set up to support connection among students (especially in the case of closing again)?

(Kentucky Department of Education, 2020, pp. 8–9)

Roles of Schools and Their Communities

The well-being of students needs to be a priority as students return to school; it will not be "business as usual."

According to a Gallup Poll, 45% of the parents indicated that being separated from classmates and teachers was a major challenge for their children (Calderon, 2020). Learning loss, lack of engagement, and limited socialization were major concerns expressed by parents that will need to be addressed whether students return to school or remain in a virtual environment.

Student Well-being in a Virtual Environment

Questions are emerging around the impact on the well-being of students as schools continue to use virtual delivery models that impact the traditional routines of physically attending school. Beyond the risk of contracting COVID-19, teachers and parents are well aware that a student's well-being affects every aspect of how he/she functions in a learning setting.

Pathways to Well-being

Dr. Joey N. Jones, the principal of Robert Frost Middle School in the Montgomery County Public Schools (Rockville, Maryland), focused on the issues related to student well-being. Robert Frost Middle School serves 1,028 students supported by 60 classroom teachers and 41 staff. The Maryland Association of Secondary School Principals (MASSP), in collaboration with the National Association of Secondary School Principals (NASSP), selected Dr. Jones as MASSP's Middle School Principal of the Year in 2019. Dr. Jones was then selected as a top-three finalist for the NASSP Principal of the Year award in 2020.

In his Narrative, Dr. Jones outlined the opportunities ahead as he and his school responded to the challenges of COVID-19, and the actions needed to bring equity for his school and community. Dr. Jones shared important lessons learned that have helped him to be a stronger and more effective leader, a teacher of teachers, and an active listener of student voices amid turbulence.

Dr. Joey N. Jones
Principal
Robert Frost Middle School
Montgomery County Public Schools
Rockville, MD

Leading for Wellness When All is Not Well: Lessons from COVID-19

Leaders are always doing one of two things—they're getting better or getting behind. I often remind my team of this mantra. The COVID-19 pandemic presented opportunities and challenges for school leaders to get better. March 13, 2020, was the day I became a better leader and marked the beginning of a new way of teaching and learning. The pandemic interrupted our school schedule and forced us home. Two weeks later, we "zoomed" into action with our Distance Learning Plan. We shifted from rigor and relevance to equity and empathy. We learned how to care from afar.

We were interrupted again, Memorial Day, May 25, 2020. The death of George Floyd at the knee of a Minneapolis police officer caused our curriculum to come alive with new meaning. The United States and the whole world woke up to the problem of systemic racism and injustice. We witnessed history and change. In the midst of these monumental moments, our students still presented needs. In some cases, the needs were intensified. Which leads me to the question: How do you lead for wellness when all is not well?

The following three lessons learned, helped me to be a consistent source of leadership in uncertain times:

- Build on the strength of your team and the established core values to meet the needs of your students.
- Allow and encourage other leaders to emerge in times of turbulence, disruption, and uncertainty.
- When in doubt, just ask! Recognize the power of student voice data.

The strength of our teams and established school core values were key foundational principles for addressing the new norms of COVID-19. Our

Instructional Leadership Team (ILT) continued to function at high levels, albeit virtually. We continued to uphold our core values:

1. Every person is valued and respected.
2. A safe nurturing environment is essential to learning (even in a virtual, online setting).
3. Success is everyone's responsibility.

To meet the needs of our students, particularly wellness needs, we had to shift our thinking from rigor and relevance to equity and empathy. Being a high-achieving school, this was easier said than done. As a leader, I constantly emphasized this message, visually and verbally, until it became a reality.

Our students and families needed time and support to figure out their own, individual situations. Equity and empathy became paramount. For example, we had to reduce the workload; alter our teaching and learning schedule; and provide flexible opportunities for engagement and support. I recall talking on the phone with a parent for over an hour. This was a necessary investment to help the parent and to help the student. In another situation, a student expressed a critical need, prior to the death of George Floyd. The student's inability to focus on learning and genuine fear was bravely proclaimed in a powerful email. Fortunately, we as a team of caring, concerned, and competent educators and counselors were positioned and available to meet the student's wellness needs and the needs of other students, too. The student was not alone. The pandemic, coupled with the social unrest and injustice, impacted my focus and concentration as well.

One of my assistant principals said, "The people who are doing the work are often the ones doing the leading." During online learning, teacher leaders, the staff development teacher, and the media specialist recognized the need for an electronic planner (e-planner). Students were accustomed to using a planner while in the school building. How would this be different in an online, virtual setting?

The e-planner was accessible via the students' Google drive and could be adapted to individual students' needs and schedules. The e-planner offered tips for reducing stress, strategies for organization, additional opportunities for connecting with staff, and guidelines for online learning

Roles of Schools and Their Communities

success. Most importantly, I was impressed with the e-planner's overall messages: *You are not alone*, *We care*, and *We are here for you*.

The success of the e-planner was captured in a student-friendly instructional video. How did all of this come about? It is important to note that the administration did not initiate this effective and timely student support. Teachers and staff identified a student need. They envisioned, inquired, collaborated, and made it happen. They energized and elevated their leadership to a different level. Students and families reaped the benefits of their efforts. Teachers and staff were doing the work. In the process, they emerged as greater leaders.

Student voice is a critical component in meeting student needs in an online learning environment. As leaders, sometimes we assume we know what students need. When in doubt, just ask! Students were asked to describe their online experiences and challenges. The student voice data was a game-changer. We asked the question, "What has been the most challenging part of online learning?" Over 70% of the students responding indicated that the number of assignments to complete was too much in the given time. Although we had reduced our instructional load, our students informed us it was not enough. Remember, we made the shift in our thinking from rigor and relevance to equity and empathy. However, our actions were not quite aligned with our thinking. Consequently, to meet student needs in their new normal, we reduced the instructional load again until we got it right. Additional findings revealed:

- Nearly 40% of students were spending three to four or more hours per day engaged in online learning.
- Nearly 56% of students said the e-planner was somewhat helpful or very helpful.
- Students appreciated teacher and staff efforts and wanted more synchronous learning opportunities that offered live, real-time student/teacher interaction.

Moving forward, educators and schools must realize that the teaching and learning model has changed. School leadership must change and adapt as well. Educators must expand their skillset and mindset to include virtual modalities. Additionally, in many cases, family dynamics must be a critical component of the conversation when leading in a virtual learning environment.

How do you lead for wellness, when all is not well? Lead with compassion, competence, core values, communication, and a community of leaders.

Dr. Jones reminded us that building team strength was important to lead in times of turbulence, disruption and uncertainty, and the necessity to change and adapt as a school leader.

Shifting Context and the Virtual Environment

In moving forward, school planning will need to evaluate and design systems to address the health and well-being of its students supported through human interaction. Schools should create clear and multiple pathways for students to make or reestablish critical connections with their teachers. Although different than in-person classroom connections, teachers in a virtual setting are able to connect with their students—see their faces, hear their voices, and create opportunities to academically engage and socially chat. As schools put in place various instructional designs and protocols to connect with students and support them, the overarching theme is that education is a human endeavor which is the most important guiding concept of it all. Midkiff (2020) describes it as being about teachers and students as people and that:

- Firstly, that learning is inherently social. Keep things personal. Finding opportunities for person-to-person interaction can go a long way.
- Secondly, while this is a tumultuous time and new measures need to be taken, keep an eye on how much you and your students can take on at one time. Be strategic about what new things you want to try.
- Thirdly, don't be afraid to encourage virtual collaboration among students. Peer support can not only help with learning, but can also go a long way to support student wellbeing.

(Midkiff, 2020, para. 27–29)

Schools have a primary responsibility for the wellness of their students whether learning in person, online, or a combination of both. This primary role of the adults in schools cannot change: schools were founded to support their students.

Leading for Tomorrow

The COVID-19 pandemic disrupted the ability for schools to carry out their many responsibilities in educating this nation's children. However, through this disruption, schools and their communities realized their joint role in supporting the social emotional needs of students.

The new work together required:

- a collective effort by schools and community agencies to understand, prioritize, and establish structures to respond;
- clarity about the social needs of students and its impact on their learning and well-being;
- new leadership teams with community memberships to lead the community's response specifically to the COVID-19 pandemic;
- targeted interventions to support the mental wellness of students especially as a result of and the lack of support when the schoolhouse was shut down;
- open communication and multiple pathways to connect with parents to understand and respond to the concerns about the health of their children.

With the COVID-19 pandemic, the collective response required by schools and community agencies underscores the need to collaborate and assume joint responsibility in the health of the children and young adults in their communities.

References

Brenan, M. (2020, April 16). Americans say COVID-19 hurting mental health most. *Gallup*. https://news.gallup.com/poll/308420/americans-say-covid-hurting-mental-health.aspx

Calderon, V. J. (2020, June 16). U.S. parents say COVID-19 harming child's mental health. *Gallup*. https://news.gallup.com/poll/312605/parents-say-covid-harming-child-mental-health.aspx

Golberstein, E., Wen, H., & Miller, B. F. (2020). Coronavirus disease 2019 (COVID-19) and mental health for children and adolescents. *JAMA Pediatrics*. 10.1001/jamapediatrics.2020.1456

Horn, M. B., Freeland, J., & Butler, S. M. (2015). Schools as community hubs: Integrating support services to drive educational outcomes. *The Brookings Institution: Discussion Papers on Building Healthy Neighborhoods, 3*. www.brookings.edu/wp-content/uploads/2016/06/Horn-Freeland-Paper-FINAL.pdf

Kentucky Department of Education. (2020, May 26). COVID-19 considerations for reopening schools supporting student and staff wellness. *Kentucky Department of Education*. https://education.ky.gov/comm/Documents/Phase%202%20Health%20and%20Wellness%20%20MC3%205-21-20%20TM%20MC.pdf

Midkiff, D. (2020, March 25). Distance learning: How do you support student wellbeing. *Firefly*. https://fireflylearning.com/blog/distance-learning-how-do-you-support-student-wellbeing/

Lanoue, P. D., & Zepeda, S. J. (2018). *The emerging work of today's superintendent: Leading schools and communities to educate all children*. Rowman & Littlefield.

Price, O. A. (2016). School-centered approaches to improve community health: Lessons from school-based health centers. *The Brookings Institution: Discussion Papers on Building Healthy Neighborhoods, 5*. www.brookings.edu/wp-content/uploads/2016/07/Price-Layout2.pdf

Reid, R. (2020, April 30). Seven things to consider when reopening communities. *ICMA*. https://icma.org/blog-posts/seven-things-consider-when-reopening-communities

7 | Leading Through the Unknown

In This Chapter...

Introduction	149
Pivoting Decisions Rapidly	150
Narrative: *System Priorities Keep You Focused During Crisis Leadership*	154
Leveraging Resources	157
Narrative: *COVID-19—Thank Goodness for Strong Finance Officers!*	159
Shifting Traditional Systems	163
Narrative: *Back to the Future?*	164
Leading for Tomorrow	169
References	170

Introduction

System leaders continued to grapple with what may be the most difficult decisions in their careers: how to best structure learning conditions that could keep students, staff, and community members safe amid the unknowns created by COVID-19. Opposing positions from internal and external stakeholders to either have schools fully open or have their schools remain fully virtual placed leaders in no-win situations. This, combined with the responsibility to create safe schools, placed tremendous pressure on school leaders on how to move forward. The famous UCLA basketball coach, John Wooden (n.d.), once commented that "Failure is not fatal, but failure to change might be." With the pandemic, schools had to change and adapt—the safety and health of students and teachers depended on the quality of those decisions.

Leaders had to pivot their thinking and actions in the midst of constantly changing and updated information with often contradictory data, triggering the need to frequently make mid-course corrections. This chapter examines the rapid nature of decision-making, leveraging resources, and the shifting of traditional systems so districts could make adaptations that fit the changing context of schooling.

Pivoting Decisions Rapidly

With no playbook on moving systems through a complete shutdown and then building plans for opening schools for fall 2020, school leaders were thrust into decision-making processes that had far-reaching consequences. At the heart of every decision was the health of children and their teachers. Let's view this new decision-making responsibility using a quick lesson in statistics. In statistics, there are two types of errors. A Type 1 Error means the patient dies. In a Type 2 Error, the patient becomes very ill but recovers. In so many ways, the decisions that leaders had to make throughout COVID-19 fluctuated between Type 1 and Type 2 with dire consequences.

There were many unknown factors that could influence outcomes requiring school leaders to be flexible, often turning their full attention in a moment's notice to act in the best interests of students, teachers, and communities. During these periods, decision-making occurred in rapid-fire succession as leaders had to change direction as new and more reliable information became available.

Closing schools in the spring of 2020 was a decision that, although heart-wrenching, was made with little hesitation. Decisions to shut down schools were made with little pushback most likely because of an understanding that the shutdowns would be short-term. However, as the shutdowns were extended, a public outcry emerged from some sectors of the community to go back to normal—the way schools functioned pre-COVID-19.

The 2019–2020 school year ended in a blur only to begin the process of making decisions related to the opening of school for fall 2020. This decision-making was complex because of changing information about the spread of COVID-19 and its impact on students and teachers. The primary question for superintendents centered on the wellness of students, staff, and community members. Most state departments of education gave latitude to individual school systems providing advice and counsel; however, they offered the caveat that opening schools would be up to the *almost sole* discretion of the system, thus shifting responsibility and liability for the decision to the system.

Systems and their leaders had to reconcile many tensions. The decision to open schools could, if the COVID-19 virus were to spike, expose students, teachers, and staff to harm. Voices across the country echoed many of the same sentiments as Dr. M. Ann Levett, Superintendent of the Savannah-Chatham County Public School System, quoted in an *Education Week* (2020, para. 3) article as saying, "It is very difficult to ignore the fact that cases [COVID-19] are continuing to rise, and they are rising exponentially… school officials are morally obligated" to act on behalf of their communities.

School districts small and large weighed the factors on whether to open their physical doors business as usual, go fully virtual, develop a hybrid model, or to delay the opening for students so teachers could better prepare for the fall of 2020. For example, Los Angeles Unified, the second-largest district in the country as well as the Chicago Public Schools, the third-largest system, closed their doors and considered opening face-to-face in the spring semester (January 2021). Regardless of the system, these decisions were typically met with mixed emotions from parents and teachers alike.

Although superintendents acted in good faith and in the instance of students *in loco parentis*, or in place of the parent, they carried the weight of the safety and welfare of students and by extension every person in the system. Their decisions alone were likely the most difficult for any district leader given the unknown of COVID-19 and the internal and external complexities of their systems and communities.

Varying levels of fear created by changing and evolving information were widespread, often creating controversy. Truth and fiction became entangled and difficult to separate, creating opposing opinions on if, or how, schools could open. While schools have always had a political element, this division over opening schools and what constituted safety if students returned birthed a fervor never experienced in education.

Politicians weighed in fiercely as President Donald Trump demanded that schools reopen in the fall with the threat of cutting funding, and Florida Governor Ron DeSantis put forth that if Walmart and Home Depot could stay open because their services are considered essential, then schools should reopen in like fashion (Sullivan, 2020). However, in reality, Walmart later required all customers and employees to wear masks in every state, and the Florida Education Association filed a lawsuit against Governor DeSantis to block the reopening of schools for fall 2020. These examples of political grandstanding were among many that further divided our nation on how schools can open, placing tremendous pressure on school leaders.

With the virus spiking widely, many working parents saw no viable options in balancing the need to work and educate their children. Many saw the need for schools to open at any cost while others were fearful of the possibility that opening schools would lead to students being lost to the COVID-19 pandemic. Furthering the complexities for school leaders was the continuous shifting of state and federal guidelines that fueled school and community confusion and exacerbated reactions from opposing groups. The decision weighed heavily on parents, much like school leaders, as they struggled to balance their children's education and safety with the basic needs of earning an income.

Nunno et al. (2020) offered counsel for leaders during "significant disruption" in identifying key challenges and offering recommendations to lead decision-making processes. Table 7.1 highlights key challenges and recommendations for framing decision-making in the context of K-12 schools.

In his Narrative, Dr. Michael Lubelfeld, superintendent of the suburban North Shore School District 112 (Highland Park, Illinois) emphasized the need to call upon others during this dark, strange, unknown, and unpredictable situation. The system serves 3,904 preK through eighth-grade students that are supported by 400 classroom teachers and 120 administrators and staff members. In 2017, he was named superintendent of the year in Lake County, IL, having previously been named the 2015–2016 National School Public Relations Association Superintendent to Watch. Dr. Lubelfeld co-moderates #suptchat—a monthly superintendent chat—and he is a published author.

Dr. Lubelfeld shared his journey about navigating difficult decisions. Using a framework based on four core principles and system priorities,

Table 7.1 Challenges and recommendations for framing decision-making

Key challenges	Recommendations for framing decision-making
Educational leaders must make decisions regarding the short- and long-term impact on educating all students based on a future of uncertainty based on a global pandemic of the 21st century.	Anchor decision-making on a framework based on the system mission and the outcomes, risks, and costs to make sound decisions in dynamically evolving situations.
For educational leaders, decision-making is significantly more complex than a traditional school or community crisis or disaster due to the multiple unknowns and the dynamics of evolving information and situations.	Adapt crisis decision-making for the long term by using safety, continuity, and resiliency criteria that reinforces and extends the core work of the district
Educational leaders, many for the first time, are making myriad stressful decisions that have a safety, health, and educational impact on students and a safety, health, and financial impact for employees.	Embrace the social realities of the pandemic, including community, emotional, and ethical criteria to help drive decisions that support students and teachers in fulfilling their roles and responsibilities.
Educational leaders must find ways to make stressful decisions in a manner that protects their students, staff, and the integrity of the function of their school district.	

Adapted from Nunno et al. (2020).

Leading Through the Unknown

he described how leaders need to unlearn and relearn in a new and different day.

Michael Lubelfeld, Ed.D.
Superintendent
North Shore School District 112
Highland Park, IL

System Priorities Keep You Focused During Crisis Leadership

In February 2020, we were getting news reports of the mysterious virus from overseas. Out of an abundance of caution, we quietly asked our janitorial subcontractor to do weekly "deep cleaning" of all hard surfaces in all ten campuses of our suburban Chicago elementary school district. Little did we know that less than a month later, we would be shutting down physical, in-person learning for the foreseeable future!

On March 12, 2020, after a special meeting of the Board of Education, we decided to close all in-person schooling due to the increase in prevalence of the COVID-19 virus in northern Illinois until April 14, 2020. This would mirror the two-week post-spring break "quarantine" period for our anticipated travelers who would travel during the planned spring break (we were loosely following higher education institutions who were making similar plans).

On March 17, 2020, the Governor of Illinois declared all public and private K-12 schools in Illinois closed through March 30, 2020 (our district was already closed through April 14). This unprecedented action was just the first of many to turn our entire school and general world into the unknown. Suffice it to say, when the Governor made his declaration, it changed the levels of significance for us, moving from one superintendent's decision to a really big deal.

System Priorities to Guide the New Work
Early on, we clearly articulated the four priorities for our leadership and work during this crisis situation:

Leading Through the Unknown

- **Priority one:** Feed our families and children.
- **Priority two:** Account for the extended safety, health, and welfare of our 4500 students and staff.
- **Priority three:** Communicate clearly.
- **Priority four:** E-learning.

These system priorities guided our decision making. First and foremost was nutrition/survival, food security. In our district, there are around 1,000 students, 25% of our student body, who depend on the school district for daily lunch and breakfast. We immediately worked with our food services team and made sure we would feed our children (we used Grab and Go breakfast and lunches). This schedule continued every day even through the summer. We also partnered with the local food bank and other local charitable groups. This also allowed us to plan for the rest of the crisis closures as well as the ultimate reopening of the system with clarity—food/survival needs superseded all other needs, including e-learning.

The priorities on general welfare, well-being, and social emotional learning for staff and students helped the community understand that we are an employer—we have more than 500 employees. As such, it was important for us to remind the community that while our "front-facing" work is teaching and learning for our 4,000 students, we are also responsible for the well-being of 500 adults. Communication is a huge priority and we shared frequent messages using email, video, the app, audio via a podcast, the live stream of board meetings, etc. We held town hall meetings, and we created Frequently Asked Questions (FAQ) documents. Our aim was to listen, learn, and lead. All of this helped us focus on the psychological and emotional needs of our people first so we could later focus on e-learning.

Lessons Learned about Leading During Disruption
We learned many lessons during the crisis period March–August 2020. We learned that humanity is far more important than any other priority. We learned that "Maslow before Bloom" is right and just—always. We learned that great leadership with relationships and communication as the foundation will always get through even the toughest of situations and the darkest of days. We learned that communication in clear, concise, short, straightforward bursts make the greatest impact.

Leading Through the Unknown

We also reaffirmed that survey data is meaningful when it is actionable. As a case in point, during the crisis learning we issued a survey to all parents, staff, and students related to e-learning. With 128 pages (yes, 128 pages) of open-ended question responses, we had our "marching orders." Starting in April and May we started to build what would become the fall return to schooling plan.

Other leadership lessons include that during the darkest, strangest, unknown, and unpredictable situations, it is wise and impactful to call upon others—to lead from a position of unity not isolation. To that end, starting on March 16, my senior staff and I met with the union president, vice president, and regional union leader each and every week to lead, plan, discuss, debate, solve problems, and in collaboration, get through this situation.

With the help of a strategic consultant from Boston, MA, we were able to assemble a 50-plus-person stakeholder planning team composed of work teams and a steering committee whose purpose was to develop plans holistically and equitably for the return to school process.

Although school systems are still facing many uncertainties as they try to resume "in-person" schooling, it is important for leaders to reach out and to get help from others to lead impactfully and effectively. Often we are faced with situations that have been done before by others, so we can look to others for their success and their failure, and we can lead with guidance. In this COVID-19 situation, our technical skills, our "known" experiences, and toolkits are not always relevant. Instead, we had to adapt and go to the unknown to create a new reality. We had to let go of some of the rituals and routines and create new ones that fit the new reality that to this date is still unfolding.

The leadership in this once-in-a-century event has caused many of us to unlearn—to approach needs in new and novel ways and to create original pathways (Lubelfeld & Polyak, 2017). To impact the future, leaders must always focus on what is best for students and their learning experiences. In our district, the motto is *Inspire… Innovate… Engage.*

Dr. Lubelfeld illustrated how important system priorities are for making decisions. Navigating the decisions school leaders needed to make brought a realization that much turbulence and stress existed when leading through multiple unknowns that necessitated changing directions quickly. Leaders made decisions based on the knowledge of their schools, communities, and current information about COVID-19; yet they realized that tomorrow may require a change in the decisions made yesterday.

Leveraging Resources

While much of the COVID-19 conversation has centered on the structures and processes that need to be in place to sustain instructional models in safe environments, little has been communicated about the details of implementation requiring re-leveraging existing resources and additional resources that could not be anticipated pre-COVID-19. Further complicating the resource issues was an expected decline in local and state taxes due to the economic impact of COVID-19. Early predictions forecast a reduction of state revenue alone to be in the 10–20% range in 2020–2021 and even more significant reductions are predicted in 2021–2022 (Griffith, 2020). While the Federal government passed the Coronavirus Aid, Relief, and Economic Security (CARES) Act (2020) designed to cover lost revenue, the money returned to schools only amounted to an average of $286.00 per student—far less than the expected loss in state and local revenues.

The big question for educational leaders is "How can we support the critical changes now requiring additional resources when we anticipate significant reductions to existing budgets?" The most logical answer for superintendents is to eliminate programs that existed pre-COVID-19. Compounding the resource challenges were new guidelines such as those for social distancing. More buses would be needed for transportation, additional classroom space for reduced class sizes, increased access to technology, additional custodial and maintenance requirements, modifications made to buildings, and the list goes on.

For school leaders, the reality that something had to be eliminated was eminent. As an example, the Randolph Public School District in Massachusetts made the decision early on that they could not sustain programs for the 2021 school year and eliminated their entire K-12 arts, music, and physical education (PE) programs and staff from their

2020–2021 budget. Nearby, Brookline Public Schools, a more affluent community, was preparing to "pink slip" 300 of their 645 teachers (McCalliss, 2020). Superintendents across the country were encountering similar scenarios that would have not only short-term impacts but also long-term implications. Dr. Daniel Domenech, Executive Director of AASA, the School Superintendents Association, predicted a dire picture that schools could not open without extra funds and the fiscal burden had become so overwhelmingly problematic that many districts had to consider returning to distance learning (Camera, 2020).

Table 7.2 illustrates data from a collaborative effort between the efforts of the Association of School Business Officials International and the School Superintendents Association (n.d.). As background, the cost analysis examined the costs involved to open the facilities of a 3,659-student school district with eight school buildings, 183 classrooms, 329 staff members, and 40 school buses (transporting at 25% capacity, or 915 students, to comply with recommended social distancing guidelines).

Table 7.2 Projected additional expenses that would be incurred in a district of 3,659 students

Area	Description	Costs
Adhering to health monitoring and cleaning/disinfectant protocols	Hand sanitizers, disinfectant wipes, thermometers, deep cleaning, and disinfectant sprayers	$116, 950.00
Hiring staff to implement health and safety protocols	Additional custodial staff, nurses, and aides	$1,232,000.00
Providing personal protective equipment (PPE)	Gloves, disposable mask for adults, and for students as needed	$194,045.00
Providing transportation and child care	Before and after school childcare, bus cleaner, and hand sanitizer	$235,144.00
TOTAL		$1,778,139.00

Adapted from the Association of School Business Officials International & the School Superintendents Association (n.d.).

Note that these costs only relate to the physical ramifications of COVID-19 and do not account for changes and their costs in the instructional program.

Mr. Robert Morales, former CFO for public school districts including Greenville County Schools (the largest school district in South Carolina), Washington, D.C. Public Schools, Cobb County Schools, Atlanta Public Schools, and Fulton County Schools cues CFOs to be ready to modify and adjust spending patterns. In addition to his work in public schools, Mr. Morales has served as the Audit Manager of the South Carolina Department of Education and the Director of State Budgeting and Finance for the Ways and Means Committee of the South Carolina House of Representatives.

Mr. Morales, in his Narrative, described the fiscal challenges that lie ahead as COVID-19 impacts revenues at the Federal, state, and local levels as well as the additional expenditures required to reopen schools. He outlined how schools need to approach a change in spending patterns as they made instructional decisions in response to the pandemic.

Mr. Robert A. Morales
Certified Administrator of School Finance and Operations (SFO)
Atlanta, GA

COVID-19—Thank Goodness for Strong Finance Officers!

As board members and superintendents of public-school districts make courageous decisions about restarting instruction in fall 2020, finance officers must be ready to adapt their budgets with each decision. There seem to be three schools of thought regarding restarting instruction. They are: 1) face-to-face instruction; 2) virtual instruction; and 3) a hybrid version of both. If parents and teachers are evenly divided with these three options, two-thirds of the stakeholders will be against any instructional decision. As such, finance officers must be ready to "modify and adjust" their spending plan with each instructional decision that is made over time. They especially have to be ready to make changes to spending patterns as new COVID-19 information emerges and community spread changes.

For example, spending for transportation will look significantly different if instruction is provided virtually.

General Fund
The general fund budget of a school district is the financial key to successful implementation of school operations and public education policy. The general fund is normally balanced or equal between anticipated revenues and projected expenditures. On occasion, depending on state or local legislation, a district's fund balance can be used to offset any reduction in revenue or overspending to maintain balance.

Revenue
Typically, revenue projections of federal, state, and local funding are determined during the annual budget process. Developing revenue projections can be particularly difficult for a school district when recessions or natural disasters affect the economy of a local community. A pandemic, like COVID-19—where major sudden unemployment occurs, retail spending stops, and the state and local municipalities take in less money—affects the ability to make accurate revenue projections.

Emergency Funds
Fortunately, the federal government traditionally provides relief packages during these times of uncertainty. In February 2009, because of the Great Recession, an economic stimulus package known as the American Recovery and Reinvestment Act (ARRA) was approved by Congress and signed into law by President Obama. In March 2020, Congress passed the Coronavirus Aid, Relief, and Economic Security (CARES) Act. President Trump signed the CARES Act on March 27, 2020. Both of these Acts provided needed resources for public school districts.

School district finance officials know that state departments of education usually provide the guidance necessary on how these federal dollars will be allocated and what spending is allowable. This is true with the CARES Act. While funding under the CARES Act is allocated based on Title 1 formulas, the funds are not Title 1. The allowable spending by school districts is much more flexible than permitted by Title 1 guidelines. "Supplement not supplant" rules among others are thus not in effect. CARES funding can be used for distance learning, facilities and equipment, meals, mental health, and supplemental learning for all students, not just Title 1 eligible students.

Political Landscape of Funding Schools Amid COVID-19

School-district finance officers should be aware that politics can play a role in special federal funding and impact the amount allocated to their public-school system. This became more evident with discussions of a school district's CARES funding being shared with private schools within a district's boundary. While various members of Congress disagreed, the U.S. Secretary of Education, Elizabeth DeVos, provided guidance and instituted rules that CARES Act funding must also go to K-12 private schools, if requested. This private-school decision reduced the amount of CARES funding to be utilized by public-school districts. As a result, public-school district finance officials must now review the invoices and contracts of private schools to both determine expenditure eligibility and to reimburse the private schools with their share of CARES funding. This is additional work for the school district finance office for public funds that are going to private schools.

In one state, the Governor announced that $32 million of $48 million received from the CARES Act would fund private-school scholarships. The use of the Governor's Emergency Education Relief Fund for this purpose appears to be contrary to that state's constitution which proclaims that "No money shall be paid from public funds nor shall the credit of the State or any of its political subdivisions be used for the direct benefits of any religious other private educational institution." Some believe the Governor made this decision when public schools failed to respond to his demand they reopen with in-person learning. This demand was made by the Governor and the leadership of the General Assembly at a state-wide press conference. Notably absent from that press conference was the elected state superintendent of education. The $32 million of federal funding, if the Governor prevails in court, cannot be counted on by that state's public-school districts even though projected revenues used to fund public education continue to decline.

Expenditures

On the expenditure side of the budget, the school board may approve spending reductions by adjusting formulas or allocations that are too generous and exceed state statute. Systems may increase spending to address

Leading Through the Unknown

human concerns such as increasing hourly rates or providing hazard (hero) pay to employees. Additionally, they may increase standard work hours for bus drivers and food service workers to prepare and distribute food, even though students are receiving instruction virtually.

It is obvious that technology expenditures for equipment and Internet access for students and staff will grow as virtual instruction increases. Additional expenditures for personal protective equipment (PPE) will also increase. In both these cases, there should be district approved standards to ensure the technology and PPE expenditures are appropriate.

A Financial Coda for District Business Officials

A school district business official needs to be aware of the ramifications to a school district's budget because of COVID-19. State revenue will take the first hit as people spend less money, reducing income and sales tax collected. Property taxes will be the next area of concern when unemployment causes an increase in unpaid property taxes or a reduction in home values. Expenditures are changing daily as school boards, administrations, and parents decide the best way to provide instruction. These variables cause uncertainty for all involved. Additional relief by the federal government remains to be seen as long as there is continued bitter dissension in the legislative and executive branches. As such, school district finance officials must be strong and focused during this turbulent time.

Mr. Morales described the current fiscal environment for school and the challenges that lie ahead. Similar to upheaval now occurring in the instructional infrastructure of schools, the landscape for managing the fiscal resources will require strong leadership and laser-like focus on how resources are added and reallocated.

Initial response to the pandemic had no price tag as district leaders did whatever was needed to maintain continuity for students and to maintain its workforce. However, as schools prepared budgets for the 2020–2021 and beyond, systems began to feel a programmatic impact with potentially dramatic reduction in programs due to fiscal restraints. With these increased costs and lost revenues, school districts will either need to find new funding streams, or make significant changes or reductions to existing programs.

Shifting Traditional Systems

System leaders were forced to examine existing systems pre-COVID-19 and to determine which practices, procedures, and policies needed to stay and which ones needed to be modified, or replaced with more appropriate ones. Leaders needed to consider not only system history and the present, but they also had to think through uncertainties and how the system would need to act swiftly with agility to pivot to the "next" change or modification. Often, the decisions by leaders were reactionary due to the changing conditions and seismic compared to traditional change processes. The rapid nature of shutting down schools, engaging in the work to patch systems (e.g., breakfast and lunch services, special education services, etc.), and supporting personnel as they implemented new systems without "blueprints" occurred mostly in an ad hoc manner. Calmness with short-term and long-term planning was needed as systems engaged in work that they never imagined they would be facing—taking temperatures when students entered the school building and moving special programs for students online, for example.

Renjen (2020) offered a perspective about leading in a crisis the magnitude of COVID-19: "Perfect is the enemy of good, especially during crises when prompt action is required" given that most schools lacked the "infrastructure to deliver perfect information or data, in real time, on operations that could be affected during an epidemic" (para. 41). A significant question that emerged as schools meandered through the challenges of COVID-19 was "What will be the new normal for schools in instructional delivery and child development and support?"

While leaders were required to make rapid changes in how schools functioned and in the services they provided, they were well aware that planning for the upcoming year was already in process. Planning now had two major stages: 1) planning in the immediate response to the COVID-19 pandemic as schools across the country closed and 2) planning for their systems to reopen in the fall complicated by changing information. Lurking behind the curtain was the emergence of a new education system.

Leading Through the Unknown

Dr. Mark A. Elgart leads us through change and scenario planning, making it clear that no manual existed for leaders to consult. Dr. Elgart is the founding President and CEO at Cognia, whose school improvement leadership is offered in over 80 countries, in 36,000 institutions that serve and support nearly 25 million students and five million educators every day. Dr. Elgart has a distinguished career of 40 years as an educational leader including time as a math and physics teacher, school principal, and chief executive leading a global, education nonprofit. He is annually recognized, both locally and internationally, as an influential leader in education due to his impact on education policy and the work of schools. He currently serves on the governing boards of Learning Forward, Springfield College, and Knowledge Alliance.

In his Narrative, Dr. Elgart provided thoughtful guidance for leading in the midst of the unknown. He laid out the challenges schools districts would face during and after COVID-19, acknowledging that traditional thinking and planning would not lead to effective solutions.

Mark A. Elgart, Ed.D.
President and CEO of Cognia
Alpharetta, GA

Back to the Future?

Every day, school leaders and their communities are contemplating an uncertain future filled with more questions than answers. Some of the questions include: How do we restart in-person schooling? How do we ensure that it is safe to attend school? How do we assure our students, parents, and teachers that it is safe? How do we reconfigure school so that health guidelines including social distancing can be maintained? What options can we provide our parents, students, and teachers who can't return to school yet? How do we operate schools with significant reductions in funding? These questions represent just a tip of the iceberg and with each question, there are myriad follow-up questions.

Unfortunately, there are no rule books or playbooks that school leaders can use to guide their planning and decision-making. However, the ability for schools to move schooling home this past spring at a moment's notice is evidence of the capacity of schools to change. Although there were clearly problems that impacted the capabilities of schools to engage all students in a stable learning environment, the dramatic shift in how schooling happened was profound. It does provide compelling evidence that if necessary, our school leaders and teachers can pivot in service to their students and parents.

The Confounding Impacts of the Pandemic

At this point, most of us are simply hoping for our daily lives to be restored including schools opening and returning to normal functioning. However, the likelihood that our schools can return to normal functioning will be severely challenged by three significant factors. These three factors will have a profound impact on how schooling happens in the present and will likely continue long into the future.

Social-emotional Impact of the Pandemic

First, the social-emotional impact of the pandemic will outlast the pandemic itself. Social-emotional impact will be a factor for students, parents, teachers, educational leaders, and communities for years to come. When will people feel safe to venture outside their home to engage the world around them? When will people feel comfortable in densely populated activities such as attending sporting events or concerts, going to church, or engaging in school? The very nature of schooling is that it is a social activity where interactions stimulate curiosity and lead to learning. The notion that children in a learning environment will adhere to social distancing is unrealistic. The impact of the pandemic on the social-emotional health of our communities will wane over time, but we cannot underestimate how it will affect the teaching and learning process of engagement.

Economic Impact of the Pandemic

Second, the economic realities of the pandemic are and will continue to significantly impact school funding. Simply put, going forward the operation of our schools will require additional funds to implement permanent changes. These changes will include new health and safety measures as well as a remote learning infrastructure. School leaders will need to reconsider how resources are allocated. Traditional distribution of resources and operational practices must change and adapt to limited and competing resources. Schooling is a labor-intensive process whereby the allocation of resources has not fundamentally changed over the last century. The vast majority of funding is spent on personnel, thereby leaving very little monies for infrastructure, training, support tools for learning, and other related areas. Additionally, the prospect of long-term, permanent increases in funding is highly unlikely.

Labor-force Impact of the Pandemic
Lastly, prior to the onset of the pandemic, teacher shortages were on the rise. The pandemic is accelerating the number of teachers leaving the profession for retirement or other jobs. In addition, the number of students matriculated in education preparation programs is dwindling. Although teacher shortages were not a consequence of the pandemic, it is increasingly more challenging to recruit and retain good teachers.

So, with concerns regarding the well-being of all the participants in the education process, insufficient funding, and growing shortages of good teachers, how can a school leader carry forward their mission in the face of such turbulence and disruption?

Scenario Planning
Traditional planning is virtually obsolete during volatile and chaotic times. There are simply too many variables that make current planning methods less reliable and unpredictable. However, leaders must be prepared for the unpredictable among the chaos. Scenario planning is the most reliable process to support a leader's preparation. In scenario planning, you capture all known variables and establish four to six scenarios using the most significant variables. The scenarios should paint a picture of the range of possibilities. Typically, aspects of two or more scenarios occur over time. The benefit to the leader is that he or she can envision these scenarios and communicate their potential to staff and the community so that stakeholders are not surprised but rather aware of possible outcomes.

The second phase of scenario planning is envisioning solutions that can address one or more of the scenarios. Leaders and their communities should identify solutions that are impervious or can adapt to the range of scenarios. In other words, what can we do that will have a lasting, positive impact regardless of the challenges we are presently facing? Specific to the pandemic, schools should take actions that are not temporary but rather invest in purposeful change that is responsive to the current situation but also an improvement for the future. If schools adopt a hybrid model of teaching in physical and virtual space, such efforts should be constructed for long-term use and benefit.

Scenario planning offers many benefits including helping leaders and their communities approach their current challenges with great optimism. Although the reality of the present is foremost in everyone's minds, having your staff and community focus on what schools can become in the future can be freeing and hopeful.

Leading, managing, and responding to the pandemic is challenging every leader in every situation. As we all struggle to manage the present, a "back to the future" approach will ultimately fail us and limit our capability to build for the future. School leaders should adopt the following steps to position their efforts for long-term improvement and benefit.

1. Understand, acknowledge, and prepare for the long-term consequences of the pandemic.
2. Engage in scenario planning that contemplates and prepares for multiple futures rather than traditional planning which plans for a single vision.
3. Adopt a "create the future" rather than a "back to the future" mindset as a leader and lead your community to the future rather than hope for a return to the past.

For some, a back to the future scenario is preferred, but the three conditions—social-emotional impact, funding limitations, and teacher shortages—will make it an extraordinary challenge, if not impossible. But then again, do we really want to recreate our past or leverage the chaos of the pandemic to create a more prosperous learning experience for every child?

Dr. Elgart painted a large picture of how education was positioned to change as schools emerged from the chaos of COVID-19. He was absolute that "a 'back to the future' approach will ultimately fail us and limit our capability to build for the future," and the that school leaders must have a new mindset for the future rather than a mindset to return to the past.

COVID-19 has caused the review of existing systems and exploration about the fundamental changes needed to support the future work of schools. Change, however, will not be on the fringes but rather on rethinking the purposes of schooling and the systems needed to make it happen. Tam and El-Azar (2020) believed education would be reshaped because "New solutions for education could bring much needed innovation… [and] could lead to surprising innovations" (para. 2, 7). Table 7.3 highlights some possible shifts of systems.

Table 7.3 Shifts in educational systems

Shifts From	Shifts To
Student access their education by attending classes in a school building	Choice—parents and student have options on how to access their education such as in face-to-face school, virtual, or mixed options
Standardized teacher and staff class ratios	Flexibility—leverage teacher and student time based on needs of students with varying size ratios
Curriculum standards developed and assigned by grade	Personalization—the curriculum is aligned to students based on their current understanding of content and skills
Set seat-time	Proficiency—student progress based on a level of comprehension
Length of school days	Access—flexible learning schedules allowing choice and 24-hour access
Teacher assignments and compensation are unified and constant	Differentiation—teacher and staff work schedules allow for new kinds of teaming, job sharing, and part-time work arrangements
Central office monitors and oversees school functions for compliance.	Service—roles, processes, timelines, and routines shift to match the needs of schools
Professional learning is designed for large groups and typically occurs on scheduled days in the calendar	Individualization—multiple professional learning opportunities using variable delivery models allow for individualized professional growth opportunities

Education has experienced many changes since its inception and some have remained while others faded. The COVID-19 pandemic will fundamentally change how students are educated in this country.

While the COVID-19 shift during spring 2020 was for most districts "crisis distance learning" because instruction "ranged from 'drive-by' course material pickups to telephone check-ins to haphazard online lesson plans and ad-hoc video conferences, all... considered low-fidelity" approaches (Ishmael et al., 2020, para. 7), the impact on the future of education looms large. Many of the crisis decisions made are playing out with long-term implications. During summer 2020, many schools, especially ones in large urban cities and towns, gave the nod to fully online instruction until January 2021. Starting dates for the 2020–2021 schools were pushed while multiple schedule configurations were rolled out with the traditional school day being altered or completely eliminated. Leaders were placed in new positions to not only ensure safety but also to bring about a systemic change not seen before.

Given the complexities of educational systems, district-level and building-level leaders are now in very tenuous positions as they make monumental decisions while maintaining coherence. Changes in education have never been easy and always had tensions to return to "normal." However, COVID-19 is like nothing ever experienced and may be the catalyst for reshaping schooling in this country.

Leading for Tomorrow

With tremendous community pressure from a wide spectrum of stakeholders regarding student safety and the return to the normality of the schoolhouse, school leaders understood the need to pivot quickly as conditions changed. For district leaders, it became clear that decisions:

- made in response to the conditions of the present COVID-19 environment held long-term implications on the educational system;
- would likely be in conflict with other local, state, and national decision-making entities;
- changed the traditions of school practices such as grading, schedules, calendars, and rituals found in the schoolhouse;

Leading Through the Unknown

- created new instructional delivery models that could likely become the mainstream;
- required shifting resources to meet safety requirements with limited budgets resulting in potential program and personnel reductions.

Leading through the unknown creates one of the most challenging landscapes for school leaders given the tensions between creating new instruction designs or returning to the traditional school model. However, the unknown has the potential of creating the new solutions schools need to fulfill their responsibility in educating all children.

References

Association of School Business Officials International, & School Superintendents Association. (n.d.). What will it cost to reopen schools? *ASBO International*. www.asbointl.org/asbo/media/documents/Resources/covid/COVID-19-Costs-to-Reopen-Schools.pdf

Camera, L. (2020, June 8). Report: No way to reopen schools safely without federal bailout. *U.S. News*. www.usnews.com/news/education-news/articles/2020-06-08/report-schools-need-a-federal-bailout-in-order-to-reopen

Coronavirus Aid, Relief, and Economic Security Act. (2020). S. 3548, 116th Cong., 2nd Sess. www.congress.gov/116/bills/hr748/BILLS-116hr748enr.pdf

Education Week. (2020, July 10). Savannah superintendent: It's still unsafe to reopen schools. *EdWeek*. www.edweek.org/ew/articles/2020/07/10/savannah-superintendent-its-still-unsafe-to_ap.html

Griffith, M. (2020, June 10). COVID-19 and school funding: What to expect and what you can do. *Learning Policy Institute*. https://learningpolicyinstitute.org/blog/covid-19-and-school-funding-what-expect-and-what-you-can-do

Ishmael, K., Heiser, R., & Payne, J. (2020, May 26). Pandemic planning for distance learning: Scenarios and considerations for PreK-12 education leaders. *New America*. www.newamerica.org/education-policy/reports/pandemic-planning-for-distance-learning-scenarios-and-considerations-for-prek12-education-leaders/introduction/

Lubelfeld, M., & Polyak, N. (2017). *The unlearning leader: Leading for tomorrow's schools today*. Rowman & Littlefield.

McCalliss, W. (2020, May 30). Massachusetts school district gets rid of art, music and PE teachers for coming school year. *World Socialist Web Site*. www.wsws.org/en/articles/2020/05/30/rand-m30.html?fbclid=IwAR3i bgj4rqJ1R7BqCXpMyaUXvjklhd_quD3E8azlbNt0XVU3o3br0q5Zkck

Nunno, T., Smith, S., Fenn, J., & Mesaglio, M. (2020, April 13). Executive decision making in the time of COVID-19. *Gartner Research*. www.gartner.com/en/documents/3983435/executive-decision-making-in-the-time-of-covid-19

Renjen, P. (2020, March 16). The heart of resilient leadership: Responding to COVID-19. *Deloitte*. www2.deloitte.com/us/en/insights/economy/covid-19/heart-of-resilient-leadership-responding-to-covid-19.html

Sullivan, K. (2020, July 7). Florida Gov. DeSantis says schools can open if Walmart and Home Depot are open. *CNN*. www.cnn.com/2020/07/10/politics/florida-desantis-walmart-home-depot-schools-reopen/index.html

Tam, G., & El-Azar, D. (2020, March 13). 3 ways the coronavirus pandemic could reshape education. *World Economic Forum*. www.weforum.org/agenda/2020/03/3-ways-coronavirus-is-reshaping-education-and-what-changes-might-be-here-to-stay

Wooden, J. (n.d.). Johnny Wooden quotes. *BrainyQuote*. www.brainyquote.com/quotes/john_wooden_378437

	Education
8	**in America**
	***Will* Change**

In This Chapter...

Introduction	172
The Journey Continues	173
Teachers, Parents, and Leaders Care	174
From System Rigidity to System Flexibility	176
Moving Forward is a Choice	177
Unspoken Responsibilities	178
Power of Community	179
A New Normal	181
Gateway to a Brighter Future	182
Narrative: *Education During the Pandemic—Lessons and*	
Opportunities	183
The Next Chapter in the Journey	187

Introduction

The journey as school districts responded to COVID-19 was unprecedented as the conditions required fundamental changes to carry forward their missions and to fulfill local, state, and national responsibilities. Amid turbulence and disruption, school leaders and teachers were thrust into positions requiring new thinking about how their districts and schools

172

Education in America *Will* Change

could effectively educate children. The COVID-19 pandemic has revealed the complexities of schools that go much deeper than the often-public view of academic test scores. Furthermore, the function of schools goes well beyond the schoolhouse walls and has a direct impact on families and the functions of their communities.

As evident throughout Chapters 1 through 7, the Narratives offered by thought leaders provide insight into how districts and schools carried forward their work and more importantly, they shined a light on the paths ahead navigating the multiple unknowns of the COVID-19 pandemic. Leading the unknown is indeed a risky undertaking but one well worth the effort moving forward with our thinking, aspirations, and actions.

This chapter looks across the previous chapters to pull out the major messages from the Narratives and to position some starting points for continuing this journey through ruptures that will undoubtedly confound the turbulence that started with the COVID-19 pandemic.

The Journey Continues

The crucial role of education took center stage as communities attempted to ready themselves in the midst of a national upheaval that impacted every aspect of life as known before COVID-19. In moving forward, the impact of COVID-19 will continue to shape the educational space as information continues to unfold. As schools ready for the future, the question of when schools will return to normal is not the right question and will not lead to effective solutions. The right question for success moving forward will center on how schools create a new normal from lessons learned during one of the most disruptive times in the history of public education in this country. More importantly, the true lessons will be about the resilience of education and the optimism required in leading our nation's schools.

Over time, the responsibility of schools to educate *all* children in this country has not changed. However, much like the rising of the phoenix, the world in which we now live and educate children must include adaptation. For this reason, what we do moving forward through this journey will be contingent on listening, learning, and leading in ways to create thoughtful and effective change.

To begin this exploration, Chapter 1 set the stage for our examination of COVID-19 in the context of schools detailing how the disruption of

173

Education in America *Will* Change

COVID-19 as well as other societal factors interrupted our focus on education. We begin our journey boldly presenting the Narratives from Dr. Susan Enfield and Dr. Stephen Joel. They both offer hope for the future and a strong resolve that as a society we can do the work necessary for schools to rebound from the distractions, ruptures, and hairline fractures experienced moving through the pandemic.

Chapter 1 is especially important in that a representative sampling of voices from students, teachers, and parents were shared. These voices illustrate the complexities and anguish they experienced and how the pressure to find solutions was often entangled by forces beyond their control or grasp. Yet, their voices carry logic that systems might consider as they communicate information, enact policies, and engage with these very special constituents.

Dr. Susan Enfield offers wisdom in the face of turbulence, disruption, and adaptation, whether it's due to a pandemic or another disruptive force. She relies on her lifelines and returns again and again to their shared core values of equity, relationships, and support. Dr. Enfield sees the all-consuming challenges of the present but also sees the hope for a bright future by applying what was learned about improving education. For Dr. Enfield, school transformation is not guaranteed without the fight for equity in designing and implementing the new programs that children deserve.

Dr. Stephen Joel reminds us of the continuous challenges facing school leaders and teachers as a result of the current pandemic. He takes to heart the dynamics of the COVID-19 pandemic and the impact of every decision that had to be made as school districts balanced the health of their students and staff with the dynamics of a charged political climate, racial unrest, and declining economics. Dr. Joel witnessed first-hand how people accomplished superhuman tasks with quick turnaround time because they knew they had to attend to the human nature of schools. He admires the ability of leaders to work through dark times with the hope of a brighter future because that is what educational leaders do.

Teachers, Parents, and Leaders Care

The unknowns of COVID-19 challenged parents, teachers, and leaders to respond quickly in addressing the needs of children. The Narratives in

Education in America *Will* Change

Chapter 2 illustrate the human nature of education and the remarkable responses to ensure that children received the support and care needed as their world was rocked when the schoolhouse doors closed.

The COVID-19 pandemic's impact on social growth and development may have more long-term impact than the predicted academic gaps on students. Dr. Grant Rivera speaks to the critical need to respond to student isolation and its impact on a student's sense of community. His approach was centered on calmness with communication and information flow that was steady and predictable. He underscores their district's success to their efforts in reaching out to families which was not happenstance or luck but rather based on a deliberate approach to be connected.

The new role of parents has created a greater disparity in the support students need to be successful in their education as parents struggle to balance work lives, act as teachers and provide needed resources. Dr. Katherine Kelbaugh provides insight about the emerging responsibility for schools to prepare for and embrace parents' new role as informed advocates for their children. As the pandemic unfolded, parents in her system were provided "new" knowledge about their role as teachers that would lead to more engagement and involvement with their child's education. She embraces the responsibility to provide stability, comfort, and strength to adolescents and the community at large.

New thinking was needed as the work of school social workers, counselors and psychologists was disrupted. Dr. Dawn Meyers speaks to the impact of this pandemic on student support systems. She detailed how families, schools, and communities collectively felt the effects of the importance of basic needs ahead of learning. Systems responded to food insecurity, anxiety and depression, and physical illness as these became paramount to learning. While the urgency of the pandemic closures created unmet needs and challenges, she sees how student support staff have opportunities to reimagine their work.

From current shifts in services, moving forward will provide opportunities for support systems to be agile and innovative, creating new tools to respond to student needs in a new educational environment. This pandemic underscores the critical role of schools for the care of this nation's children. New systems and supports are required in meeting the emerging social and physical health as schools work to support students and parents.

From System Rigidity to System Flexibility

Educational systems have been notoriously characterized as static systems where change is assessed in months and years versus the technology environment that changes by the day. However, this stronghold on the traditional educational delivery systems was penetrated in hours when COVID-19 invaded communities across the country. Narratives in Chapter 3, address an unfamiliar and immediate disruption that thrusted schools into an action of rapid change.

Amid this crisis-level reaction in response to COVID-19 was an emerging new realization that schools would likely never return to their often-static existence. Dr. Donald Robertson, Jr. foresees this experience to forever change their school district requiring agility and adaptability, with the use of technology to meet staff, student and family needs becoming commonplace. He underscores innovative leadership founded on what leaders say and do and the need for school leaders to listen more, speak less, and recognize this is a challenge requiring everyone to think and act differently at one time or another.

As schools prepare for a return to school buildings, the logistics range from building safety requiring retrofitting and detailed cleaning to new protocols for transportation and health screening. Dr. Douglas Huntley reminds us that the learning environments created in schools must provide a sense of stability and connectedness, requiring safe and healthy school environments that are flexible to accommodate new instructional designs. He implores leaders to focus on school facility designs and to be prepared for emerging forces not always known such as in the current pandemic.

Leaders will be required to rethink the change framework for their districts and create processes that can support the agility for school programs for the future. Dr. Brian Troop emphasizes the need to collectively navigate change in their school community by asking key questions:

- What knowledge, skills, and dispositions do graduates need to *reach their full potential* in life?
- What do we know about how to engage students toward the development of these traits?
- What type of educational program(s) do we have the capacity to deliver?

Education in America *Will* Change

Dr. Troop embraces the concepts that the world is rapidly changing and the impact of the COVID-19 pandemic will continue to reshape society and transform many aspects of school communities.

The reality is that schools returning to "normal" will not happen. However, change creates new opportunities to invoke innovative systems that support children being successful in the context of *their* world. New thinking contrary to the static nature of schooling across the country can bring new options for children, if we choose to do so.

Moving Forward is a Choice

One of the significant takeaways from the changes incurred in response to COVID-19 has been the emergence of programs different from the mainstream of instructional delivery in a classroom. The national movements defined by federal and state mandates such as high-stakes testing and school rankings no longer defined the work of schools. The Chapter 4 Narratives address changes in instructional models and new models no longer considered an as alternative but rather an option for children and teachers.

When schools shut their doors, the concept of school days and hours along with class periods and set times changed dramatically in ways that will have a long-term impact. Dr. Mary Elizabeth Davis addresses the need to pivot from traditional schedules as schools learned quickly that traditional schedules in an online delivery model did not work. In systems planning, she embraced the changes in how central offices functioned to support schools by developing "new playbooks" to build local routines and to detail preparations for every department in her system. While she wanted her district to celebrate and say good-bye to 2019–2020, Dr. Davis clearly recognized the need to say hello and embrace 2020–2021.

The move to remote learning was difficult and required teachers to unlearn many of the practices used in the traditional classroom settings. Mr. Jeff McCoy realized early in the pandemic that it would vastly change how they do business. While his initial reactions included concerns about undoing the district's creative approaches, Mr. McCoy sees opportunities to strengthen the system's work using online learning systems. Mr. McCoy used disruption to reimagine the system's current efforts while embracing the need for student socialization as much as he believed that some students learn better in an online environment.

Education in America *Will* Change

In whatever combination, whether face-to-face or virtual, teachers needed to engage their students showing their resolve to care for them. Dr. Susan Stancil emphasizes the foundational need for a caring culture and strong relationships to be in place to withstand any disturbance that disrupts them from serving their students and families. She focused on keeping faculty and staff connected and continued building a positive and healthy culture that inspired trust. Dr. Stancil understood that relationships matter.

In moving beyond this pandemic, one view would align to the same philosophical traditions that are currently foundational to educating the students in this country or one can examine what was different during this pandemic and return to a new normal that is truly different and brings new hope in addressing the inequities that have existed since beginning of public education. Change is distilled to a choice.

Unspoken Responsibilities

What emerged when the schoolhouse doors closed was a stark understanding of the role schools played in providing the support children needed as they grow and mature into adulthood.

Although a challenging responsibility before COVID-19, schools across the country now needed strategically to address the short- and long-term impact of the pandemic on their student's social development. Narratives in Chapter 5 focus on social emotional supports and how schools pivoted to respond to these needs.

The gaps created by COVID-19 to student social emotional development and learning were of critical concern for school leaders and teachers. Dr. Armand Pires describes how the health pandemic left everyone feeling out of balance as they moved from a traditional school experience in early March, 2020. His district focused on two areas that were inextricably connected: mitigating educational regression and supporting students' social and emotional wellness. The importance of both student academic learning and social and emotional wellness were clear from the onset and required coordinated planning for success. Opportunities for students and teachers to engage in ways to build trusting and effective relationships were developed based on personalized student support services.

With diminished social and emotional support provided for students at school, new systems were required to maintain a high level of support especially in a virtual environment. Dr. Jill Baker reflects on her district's response by realizing a need for a new understanding of the terms "pandemic" and "unprecedented." The issue for Dr. Baker was not about distributing technology but rather recreating the connection, inspiration, and motivation ignited by human contact. Dr. Baker envisions now how planning for "storms" like COVID-19 will require keeping equity at the center of decisions, listening to students' voices, developing strong teams, and creating support systems for every individual in the system.

The emotional strain on teachers to create a fundamentally new mind shift was challenging; however, the commitment by teachers and their ability to move through their own challenges ensured the right supports were in place for their students. Mr. Rich Merlo connects the work of his district to the new work required during COVID-19. While the driving force for the district embraced developing ownership of learning, the COVID-19 pressed thinking to new levels for teachers and leaders. The district-built correlates to ensure interpersonal communication continued to build relationships and to support a student's total emotional, mental, and spiritual well-being. Mr. Merlo embraced the approach that they needed to understand the problem and to own the solutions sharing that it was "our ability to 'own our story.'"

The breadth of the work and responsibilities of schools in the social emotional development of this nation's children has been fully revealed during this pandemic. In moving beyond COVID-19, the most significant area for policy-makers and communities is to get beyond the view that the success of schools is based on high test scores by realizing that systems and schools must balance social emotional well-being with expectations for high performance.

Power of Community

The work of schools and the responsibilities of local government, businesses, and community agencies became galvanized in ways unfamiliar to each entity. Schools and communities could no longer work in isolation regardless of past practices, experiences, policies, and politics. They could reopen only through collective solutions to fulfill each organization's

Education in America *Will* Change

responsibilities while keeping everyone safe. Chapter 6 Narratives speak to the relationships now needed to meet the totality of educational and health needs of not just schools, but for their communities.

Schools needed to work directly with community agencies in developing plans that will likely redefine relationships and allocation of resources. Dr. Calvin Watts speaks to the need for clarity between organizations of the problems they collectively were trying to solve and the complexities of the solutions. He underscores the importance of comfort and strength in numbers. At the forefront in seeking solutions, Dr. Watts upheld and supported the values of diversity, equity, and inclusion to move further toward educational justice. Dr. Watts valued the need for school leaders to embrace the inclusion of community by reflecting on their roles and responsibilities related to how they support every student, family member, and community member.

Schools learned much about their roles and responsibilities in supporting children and the gaps in student support. Dr. Nardos King shares that schools and communities must learn from mistakes of the past to do better for their children. Dr. King learned of greater inequities in their schools that must be addressed, the incredible commitment of teachers and school leaders, and that, above all else, students were counting on them. In disasters like COVID-19, the right voices must be around the table with consistent and clear communication and interact with grace to all, for ultimately, students are counting on all of us.

The developing scenarios of how schools would open in fall 2020 highlighted the disparities and inequities furthering the requirement to work collectively as one community in developing new solutions to new problems. Dr. Joey Jones shifts his thinking from a focus of rigor and relevance to one of equity and empathy. He recognized the need for students and families to have time and support as they strived to navigate new situations and again emphasized the paramount need for equity and empathy. Dr. Jones understood that leading for wellness when all is not well requires leading with compassion, competence, core values, communication, and a community of leaders.

In many ways, this pandemic exposes the gaps in school and community support that are needed to address the existing and widening inequalities felt by students, parents, and community members. In moving forward, the roles and functions within communities and schools cannot be "business as usual" nor can the conversations be insular among entities

Education in America *Will* Change

within the community. Now, more than any time in the history of education, is the time for schools and communities to act as one for their children.

A New Normal

The responsibility felt by leaders in educating this nation's children has never before carried the weight of COVID-19. School leaders across the country needed to balance the intense pressure created by opposing positions on whether it was safe to open schools with their own responsibility to ensure the safety of all children. Narratives in Chapter 7 forecast that change must be on the horizon as schools will never return to the same place as pre-COVID-19.

The thought of returning to a new normal: a place different from traditional schools requires clear communication and making difficult decisions in moving forward. Dr. Michael Lubelfeld illustrates how he reached out to his community and emphasized the priorities for the school district. He embraced the role of schools in protecting the general welfare, well-being, and social and emotional learning for staff and students. Dr. Lubelfeld leveraged leadership relationships and communication to move through the toughest situations while understanding that many existing rituals and routines were no longer effective, requiring the creation of new ones that fit the new reality. Dr. Lubelfeld understood the need to "unlearn" much that he had learned in leading schools and systems.

As schools implemented changes to open schools for the fall of 2020, the differences in available resources began to be exposed as fiscally challenged districts struggled. Mr. Robert Morales makes clear the need to change spending patterns as new COVID-19 information emerges and community spread changes. He predicts that while school districts are fiscally challenged now, the fiscal picture will likely get worse. The tax base for funding schools will be negatively impacted by the changes in the economy while state and federal money may or may not be forthcoming. And if so, there is the potential that resources will be connected to political agendas. School leaders will feel new challenges in the pandemic as decisions are made to eliminate or change programs based on new and emerging fiscal priorities.

Education in America *Will* Change

The COVID-19 pandemic highlights how uncertainties of future disruptions can impact schools, requiring agility to respond. Dr. Mark Elgart describes the significant impact on systems across the country as school leaders and their communities contemplate an uncertain future filled with more questions than answers. As school systems move forward, Dr. Elgart predicts that the social and emotional impact, the economic impact, and the labor force impact will have a profound influence on how schooling operates in the present and continues long into the future. For Dr. Elgart, the success of education in America will be in the hands of school leaders who have a new mindset of moving forward and not returning to yesterday.

The tensions in this unknown time have created much turbulence and uncertainty as leaders understand a need to redesign schools as they move forward. However, the road to change will not be an easy one and will require new mindsets for every stakeholder as districts rethink how they fulfill their responsibilities to educate their children. At stake today is the national responsibility to educate all children.

Gateway to a Brighter Future

Educational reform is not new to the American educational system. Most reform movements targeted a better future for all students with leaders hurrying to implement legislation and policies with the creation of new programs and practices. While these efforts pressed changes in education and reformed schools in some ways, the reality was that many students were failed by the very systems forced to comply with these externally driven mandates.

While many concerns paint a gloomy future with widening achievement gaps, Dr. Daniel Domenech, Executive Director of the AASA the School Superintendents Association, portrays optimism that this horrific COVID-19 journey can, if we choose, lead to a brighter future.

Dr. Domenech was elected President of AASA in 1998 and was chosen as the Executive Director of AASA in 2008. In 2002, an American Flag was flown in his honor over the US Capitol in recognition of his contributions to education after 27 years as a school superintendent. AASA, the School Superintendents Association, has over 10,000 members and represents school superintendents nationwide. Its mission is to be advocates on behalf of the children served by our schools and to support the work of its members and to enhance their professional development.

Many past reform movements in education have resulted in inconsistent results with mostly fringe changes in educational design. Dr. Daniel Domenech forecasts how the COVID-19 pandemic has the potential to change the face of education.

Daniel A. Domenech, Ph.D.
Executive Director
AASA, the School Superintendents Association
Arlington County, VA

Education During the Pandemic — Lessons and Opportunities

Education has not changed dramatically since I began my career as a sixth-grade teacher in New York City. While there certainly have been improvements and many districts and schools have innovative programs, that innovation has not found its way into as many districts as it should. There is no better time than now, amid a life-changing pandemic, to change the face of education.

After three years in the classroom, I successfully applied for an administrative position with the Board of Cooperative Educational Services (BOCES) in New York, an intermediate agency providing services to 56 school districts on Long Island.

As Director of Redesign Programs, I was charged with scouring the country in search of innovative education initiatives and introducing those programs to our component school districts. My team and I traveled to the Kettering Foundation in Dayton, Ohio, to investigate their individualized education program, a precursor to today's personalized learning initiative. In Flint, Michigan, we received a first-hand look at their community-in-school program, the beginning of wraparound services for students.

In San Francisco and New York City we visited bilingual classrooms, a growing trend in the education of English as Second Language students. We observed education in open classrooms—a fad in which classrooms in newly constructed school buildings did not have walls. We reviewed our own Mother Interaction Program at BOCES, which trained parents to be their child's first teacher.

Education in America *Will* Change

It was a fantastic experience and one that shaped my vision for the school districts I served as a Superintendent. During my 27 years in the position in four districts, I drew upon my experiences and introduced many of those innovations to my schools.

The first district that hired me as Superintendent did so because they had incurred a significant budget deficit and needed an innovative solution. I reorganized the district using the Princeton Plan model I had seen during my BOCES years: K–3 primary centers, 4–6 intermediate schools, 8–9 middle schools, and a 9–12 high school. The new model allowed for the closing of three facilities. The savings overcame the deficit.

In other districts I introduced childcare, preschool programs, full-day kindergarten, bilingual programs, non-graded programs, individualized learning, year-round schools, and more.

Although I retired from the superintendency 16 years ago, in my current post as the Executive Director of AASA, the School Superintendents Association, I continue to advocate for change.

Questioning Today's Education

Here we are, in the 21st century, yet our schools continue to adhere to practices that date back to the 20th century and earlier. We still organize our schools by grade levels even though we know that children of the same age do not all have the same abilities. Teachers continue to deliver the same lesson to the entire class even though, on average, a third of the class cannot keep up and a third of the class already knows the material.

Children are pulled out of classes for remediation, thus ensuring that they are missing lessons and falling further behind. Children fail and are forced to repeat the grade in its entirety even though they have already mastered much of the material. We create barriers that prevent many of our minority and economically disadvantaged students from gaining access to quality programs. The students who need school the most are often suspended or expelled.

Seat-time requirements demand students to be in the classroom a prescribed number of hours to get credit for the course even though competency-based assessments could show that they have mastered the material sooner. School calendars still include months-long summer vacations even though we are fully aware of the learning loss that occurs

184

Education in America *Will* Change

during students' time away from the classroom. We fail to recognize that many of our students have issues outside of the school that prevent them from learning. We continue to focus only on the academics and ignore the social and emotional needs of the child, and we wonder why we still have achievement gaps.

Education in Pandemic Times

All of us that have labored during our careers to transform education recognize the opportunity that the pandemic presents in terms of making the changes that we sought but could not sustain. What lessons can we learn and what opportunities can be created by the crisis?

Flexible Scheduling

The pandemic caused havoc to school calendars, closing schools in the spring, delaying openings in the fall, and robbing students of crucial instructional time. A more flexible calendar that extends year-round would allow for school closures and provide additional days necessary for students to make up for the loss of learning during the pandemic. A flexible calendar based more on hours in school rather than on days would also allow for a shortened school day to accommodate additional remote learning from home. This may be the time to be rid of the traditional school calendar, transition to year-round schooling, eliminate seat-time requirements, and reconsider the number of days students are required to be physically in school since remote learning is now a reality. This can be the end of the "edifice complex," the notion that learning can only occur in the school building.

Personalized Learning

Rather than relying on remediation programs, after-school programs, summer school, or the repetition of a grade level, personalized learning is a 21st-century solution to keeping students on track toward graduation. As districts and teachers become more adept at using technology, they can provide a personalized education plan for each student to assess where the student is and prescribe a program that moves the student from that point forward.

This is also an effective approach for the more independent, advanced students, so they are not held back in their progress. Personalized learning

Education in America *Will* Change

gives the students more responsibility for their education, more choice, and the ability to progress at their own pace.

As the quality of online offerings improves, the use of synchronous and asynchronous instruction frees up teachers to work with smaller groups of students in person while the other students engage in online learning, either within the classroom or at home. This facilitates personalized learning and helps struggling students catch up when they are given priority for more time with in-person instruction.

Cost Savings

School funding has historically been a lower priority for our elected officials and consequently school budgets are rarely adequate. Even during the pandemic, educators could not convince Congress to allocate the dollars schools needed to operate safely. Because remote learning makes it possible for students to learn anywhere, districts with overcrowded schools can adhere to the hybrid model and no longer rely only on the expenditure of millions of dollars on costly building expansions or renovations. They can further economize by using learning management platforms and content developed at the state or regional levels, as some states already offer, rather than each district having to develop their own. Education Service Agencies can expand on the cooperative services already in place for their component districts and further realize greater savings.

If personalized learning is effectively implemented, remediation programs, after school, summer school, pull-out programs, and grade repetition would no longer be necessary. How much money would that save?

Righting Inequality

The pervasive inequity in our schools was exposed during the pandemic as wealthier districts that had already provided every student with a laptop, trained the teachers in online instruction, and purchased the platforms to offer it, successfully pivoted to online instruction. Economically disadvantaged districts did not have the equipment, software, or training, and consequently their students suffered. The lack of Internet connectivity in many of the homes added to the disparity.

There is the opportunity to eradicate these inequities by providing greater federal funding to school districts in impoverished communities. The financial contribution from the Federal government has seldom exceeded 10%. The need to ensure that all students have access to remote learning,

Education in America *Will* Change

even after the pandemic, will require a sustained level of funding well above 10%. It will also require that the distribution of Federal funds not be diluted by attempts to fund non-public schools. Privatization attempts will continue to take away funding from the children that need it.

There is also the opportunity to remove the barriers that deny students access to a quality education. There is the opportunity to recognize that every child should learn and progress at the rate appropriate for them. There is the opportunity to fully leap into the 21st century, leave cumbersome traditions behind, and allow all children to realize their full potential. Exclusionary practices that deny students admission into honors programs, gifted programs, advanced placement programs, and other high-quality offerings need to be examined. Disciplinary practices that take students out of the education system, rather than keeping them in, need to be revised.

Those of us that have attempted to make these changes bear the scars we have received for our efforts. We also bear the satisfaction for whatever successes we achieved. This pandemic may well be the worst event of our lifetime, but it may also be the gateway to a brighter future for education.

In many ways, Dr. Daniel Domenech poses a challenge to all educators across the country. He urges us to rely on our experiences with the chaos of COVID-19 as an opportunity to rethink education for a new future. While the response to shutting the schoolhouse doors and moving to virtual environments has often been chaotic and inconsistent, the outcomes should lead as the basis for the future. The call to action to lead into the future is, in large part, by asking new and different questions about delivery systems and practices. From such leadership, there is a better chance for creating schools more readily able to adapt to systems borne from change and turbulence. This call to action is the motivation to explore some of the possibilities as we move into the next chapter of the journey.

The Next Chapter in the Journey

As schools walk through the ongoing journey to educate students, leaders and teachers will steer their communities to reimagine what education can become. Although we do not have a playbook to guide our decisions, we do have a great opportunity to learn from the turbulence of the COVID-19 pandemic and other societal disruptions. We have seen systems across the country respond, adapt, and create clarity and resilience as they moved their districts forward.

The Emerging Reality

Fall 2020 continues. Teachers, leaders, and parents are unraveling many unintended consequences of life in schools, home, and community that continue to blur. This blurring brings to light new systems and refinements that will enable schools to improve well beyond the challenges of COVID-19 (e.g., community health and wellness partnerships, multiple instructional delivery models, high-stakes testing, social emotional supports for students and staff, etc.). Before COVID-19, the picture of schools portrayed by media outlets was typically about low test scores, discipline, and inadequate teachers. Given the lack of a universal school system context, the public was often quick to make judgments based on data that did not reflect the work of the schools and their conceptions of what a "good" education looks like.

Although social media made the work of districts and schools even more visible, the news did not always portray teachers, parents, and leaders in a positive light. Given the lack of a universal school system context, the public is often quick to make judgments based on their conceptions of schools and what a "good" education looks like. Moreover, the public had the luxury of playing sideline critics about schools' decisions, often requiring immediate responses to changing conditions. Teacher positions on whether they felt safe or not in schools created much political banter of differing positions across communities and states. However, the emerging difference in opinion from pre-COVID-19 was seeing heroes for many reasons other than high test scores. Teachers were being heard, talked about, and hailed for their personal professionalism and commitment to the well-being of their students.

Leading from the Inside

Through the noise of divergent public opinions, we are confident the public now realizes the work of teachers and leaders often not visible. Through the Narratives of thought-leaders, we were fortunate to capture front-line views of what systems did, and how they mobilized these actions to help pave the way into the unknown future of their school systems given the nefarious nature of the COVID-19 virus.

The Narratives presented in this book allowed us to look inside systems and their schools to

1. shine the light brighter on issues of equity;
2. see how teachers and leaders adapted to meet present needs with an eye to the future; and,
3. illustrate how systems redefined their work based on multiple changing conditions as the pandemic persisted.

The Narratives illustrate that context matters a great deal in how leaders approached adaptation based on the needs of their systems. The systems whose journeys are presented through their Narratives illustrate new thinking situated across broad geographical locale, size, and the overall demographics.

Moving Forward in an Unknown Space

For schools, the term *journey* represents an expedition into unfamiliar territory that will continue as the events of COVID-19 play out for the next several years. It is through these early glimpses presented by system and school leaders that we have a head start into unpacking the many questions and thorny issues that can result in new opportunities for education.

As we end our work in this book, we fully realize that its content does not portray, in any fashion, an ending or a finish-line stake in the ground. Rather, the messages speak to the work *in progress* by experts in the field whose descriptions are critical guideposts in moving forward in an unknown space.

The COVID-19 pandemic may, in fact, have the greatest impact on our education systems than any planned reform could expect. The pains of children, parents, teachers, and school leaders have been like no other in the history of public education. However, these hurtful times may lead to educational reform that can truly meet the needs of all children in this country. The future of education and its success lies solely on how we move forward in this journey.

Questions for Change

To steer the journey, systems and their schools need to look at what they aspire as the sum toll of their efforts:

Do we want to return to an educational system known before COVID-19, *or* do we want to reimagine school systems that are built on addressing the totality of the needs for *all* children in the world in which they will live?

What we have learned in the preceding months about the role of schools during this pandemic prompted us to ask several critical questions to assist systems and their communities to move the discussion forward.

1. Will the term "traditional school" be defined only as entering the schoolhouse in the morning and leaving in the afternoon followed by completing homework? OR, can schooling be defined through multiple ways to access information and construct learning?
2. Will the effectiveness of schools that have a primary focus on meeting the health and developmental needs of students have a similar level of effectiveness as schools with high academic test scores? OR, will schools remain relegated to a rating and number?
3. Will educating our nation's children rest squarely on schools? OR will educating children rest squarely on their community, state, and country?
4. Will schools be run by experts in the field? OR will schools be run by people voted in political office?

There are many more questions as presented here and in the chapters. Unfortunately, we do not have the luxury of answers, but we have the utmost confidence that the answers will emerge. The answers to these questions and more will evolve as practices inform system judgments. We hope that when we can see more clearly through this pandemic that the voices and sentiments of practice will inform a broader policy arena for the future.

Index

Note: Page numbers in *italics* indicate figures, and page numbers in **bold** indicate tables on the corresponding pages. Authors in *italics* appear in Narratives throughout the book.

accountability 27–28, 77
achievement gap 32–33, 182, 185
adaptation 2, 52, 69, 82, 150, 173–174
Adler, J. 66
Alliance for Excellent Education 101
Amanti, C. 44
American Association of School Administrators 15, 158, 182–184, 187
American Federation of Teachers 15
Anderson, S. 63–64
Arruda, W. 93
Arseneault, L. 102
Ascione, L. 52
Association of School Business Officials International 158

Bailey, R. 106
Baker, J.A. 109, 111, 114, 179

basic needs 30, 42, 45, 51–52, 116, 175
Belsky, D. 102
Biden, J. 9, 10
Blackburn, S. 51
Bloch, E. 34
Brackett, M. 108, 122
Brenan, M. 33, 141
Breunlin, E. 26
Brion-Meisels, G. 106
Brown, A. 20
Brown, B. 120
Brush, K. 106
Butler, S.M. 129

Calderon, V.J. 141–142
Californians for Justice 113
Calloway, A. 65
Camera, L. 158
Candeias, A.A. 100
CASEL 107, 110
Caseman, K. 63–64

191

Index

Caspi, A. 102
Castro, F. 65
Caulfield, J. 63
Centers for Disease Control and Prevention 15, 59
change and conventions of schooling 4, 12, 20, 75, 82–83, 85–87; assessment 26, 53, 55, 75–77, 184; human endeavor 30; online learning 3, 20, 33, 41; rituals and routines 25; school calendar 77, 184–185; shifts in educational systems **168**; schoolhouse 82–83; system flexibility 176–177; teaching 19, 87; time 77; traditional and virtual teacher work models **88**; virtual environments 13, 19, 27–28, 87
Charns, M. 65
child abuse 39–40, 128
Child Abuse Prevention & Legal Treatment Act Reauthorization of 2010 40
child development *see* social and emotional development
Cipriano, C. 108, 122
cleaning protocols 3, 58–60, 63, 131, 154, 158, 176
Cognia (Alpharetta, GA) 164
Cole, D. 15
Collins, C. 120
Collopy, R. 41
Committee on Education & Labor 3
community agencies and organizations 65, 129, 135–136, 138, 147; hubs 128–129

community relationships 128–129; emerging community roles 128–130; power of 179–181
compensatory support 41
context of COVID 2, 68–69, 146–147, 150, 188, 189; disruption 9–11, 71, 171–173; Donald J. Trump 9–10, 13, 15, 152, 160; police actions 9–10; political 10; racial unrest 9, 128, 174; unspoken responsibilities 178–179
contingency planning *see* scenario planning
Cook, N. 65
Corcoran Joint Unified School District (Corcoran, CA) 117
Coronavirus Aid, Relief, and Economic Security Act (CARES Act) 3, 33, 157, 160–161
Couros, G. 2
Court, B. 89
COVID slide 26, 32, 39
covidiot 10
Cristóvão, A.M. 100
custodial 57–58, **59**, 157

Davis, M.E. 78, 82, 177
decision making 9, 155; challenges and recommendations **153**; engaging stakeholders 70; rapid nature 19, 68, 83, 150
Dede, C. 83
Department of Education 40
DeSantis, R. 14, 15, 152
DeVos, B. 15, 161
Dewey, J. 102
Dickson, N. 43, 102

digital access 41, 61–62,
76; closing digital divide
61–62; communication 94;
environment 90
disequilibrium 7–8, 16
disinfecting *see* custodial
disruptions 1–2, 4, 9–10, 116–117,
128, 182; attendance 28, 31, 69,
131, 139; daily routines 17, 94;
emotional 109
Domenech, D.A. 158,
182–183, 187
Dove Creek Elementary School
(Statham, GA) 89–90
Durlak, J.A. 100, 107

Education Reimagined 57
Education Trust-New York 34
Education Week 151
Ehmer, C. 94
El-Azar, D. 168
Elgart, M.A. 164, 167, 182
Elsen-Rooney, M. 45
Emery, C. 107
emotions *see* social emotional
learning
entry plans 129, 134
Ephrata Area School District
(Ephrata, PA) 67, 68
equity 6, 9, 33, 76, 111, 113,
133, 142, 144–145, 174, 179,
180, 189; digital access
32, 61–62
equilibrium 95–96
Every Student Succeeds Act 77

facility design 60, 63, 80, 82, 176;
social distancing 13, 18, 57–**58**,

62–63, 84, 86, 108, 116, 141,
157–158, 164
Fairfax County Public Schools (Falls
Church, VA) 136–137
Fasso, G.I. 25
Fenn, J. 152–153
Fisher, D. 114
Flannery, M.E. 16
Flinn, S.K. 20
food insecurity 28, 64, 175; bus
deliveries 3
Foothills Education Charter High
School (Athens, GA) 41–42
free and appropriate public
education (FAPE) 40
Freeland, J. 129
Frey, N. 114
funding 3, 10, 13, 33, 152,
160–163, 165–166, 181,
186

Gao, N. 40
Garcia, A. 108
Gavin, J. 40
Golberstein, E. 141
González, N. 44
Greenville County Schools
(Greenville, SC) 83–85, 159
Griffith, M. 157

Hallum, M. 14
Hancox, R.J. 102
Hares, S. 33
Harrington, H. 102
Harris, K. 9
Hattie, J. 114
health 42, 127; clinics and
partnerships 136; school health

Index

considerations **65**; services 3, 56, 63–64
healthy children 135
Heiser, R. 169
Henry County Schools (McDonough, GA) 78–79, 82
Hickman, A. 93
high-stakes testing 76–77, 177, 188
Highline Public Schools (Burien, WA) 5–6
Hill, D. 20
Hill, L. 40
HIPAA 64
Horn, M.B. 129
Houts, R. 102
human connections 75, 88; virtual world 89
Huntley, D. 60, 63, 176

Individual Education Plans (IEPs) 39–40, 54–55
inequality 186–187
infrastructure 3, 57, 62, 163, 165
instructional models and delivery 83–84; digital 41, 80, 83, 89, 92, 95; hybrid 34, 151; learner-centric virtual environments **57**; online lessons 25; shifts in teaching 18, 50, 83
Ishmael, K. 169

Jacobson, L. 39, 41
Jarrett, L. 33
Jensen, L. 39
Joel, S. 10–11, 13, 174
Jones, J.N. 142–143, 146, 180
Jones, S. 106

Kahn, J. 106
Kamenetz, A. 39
Karlsberg, R. 66
Kelbaugh, K. 35, 38, 175
Kent School District (Kent, WA) 129–130, 132–133
Kent, C. 94
Kentucky Department of Education 141
Kimberly, J. 65
King, N.E. 136–137, 140, 180
Krueger, N. 116
Kuhfeld, M. 33
Kutylo, B. 71

Lanoue, P.D. 115, 136
Laura, J. 20
leadership 145, 154 *see* decision making; sustainability 66–67
learner centric approaches **57**
learning gaps 33, 72; loss 77
learning spaces *see* instructional models and delivery
Lendrum, A. 107
leveraging resources 157–158
LGBTQ+ 39
Lincoln Public Schools (Lincoln, NE) 10–11
Local Education Agency (LEA) 40
Long Beach Unified School District (Long Beach, CA) 109, 111, 114
Lubelfeld, M. 152, 154, 156, 181

Magee, M.P. 2
Mahoney, J.L. 100, 107
Marietta City Schools (Maretta, GA) 26–27, 29
Maslow, A.H. *31*, 155

Maslow's Hierarchy of Needs *31*, 155; connecting with students 116; developing positive relationships 31; security *31*; sense of belonging 27, 94

Massachusetts Department of Elementary and Secondary Education 103

McCalliss, W. 158

McCoy, J.C. 83–84, 87, 177

McIntyre, J. 106

McLeod, S. *31*

medically fragile students 63, **65**

Medway Public Schools (Medway, MA) 102–103

mental health services for students 7, 20, 43, 63, 105; school clinics and health partnerships 136; support 140–142

Merlo, R. 117, 120, 179

Merrill, S. 121

Mesaglio, M. 152–153

Meyers, D. 41–42, 45, 175

Midkiff, D. 146

Miller, A. 76

Miller, B.F. 141

Mirra, N. 108

mobile devices 25

Modan, N. 41

Moffitt, T.E. 102

Moll, L. 44

Montgomery County Public Schools (Rockville, MD) 142–143

Morales, R.A. 159, 162, 181

Mundy, K. 33

National Association of School Nurses 64

National Association of School Psychologists 102

National Education Association 100

Nelson, K. 114

new systems 25, 56 *see also* instruction; custodial 58–**59**; facility designs 60; health services 63–**65**; technology 57; trajectories 16; transportation 57–**58**

No Child Left Behind 77

North Shore School District 112 (Highland Park, IL) 152, 154

Northwest Evaluation Association 77

NRT Bus Inc 57

Nunno, T. 152–153

Oconee County School District (Watkinsville, GA) 90

Oldfield, J. 107

Page, S. 108

parents 2, 16, 18, 37–38, 92, 140; challenges 20, 34, 39, 152; new roles 3, 34, 91, 95, 175; support 34–35, 121

Payne, J. 169

Pence, M.R. 9, 13

Pires, A. 102–103, 106, 178

Pitas, N. 94

Polyak, N. 156

Pomrenze, Y. 33

Poulton, R. 102

Price, O.A. 136

Puentedura, R.R. 112

Index

quarantine 5, 17, 154

Rafaeli, S. 94
RAINN 39
Rechavi, A. 94
Reid, R. 134
relationships 4, 17, 26, 28, **31**, 88, 92–93, 95, 105; student development 31, **57**; virtually 89–90, 100
Renjen, P. 163
Rethink 122
revenue 152, 160, 162
rituals and routines *see* change and conventions of schooling
Rivera, G. 26, 30, 175
Robert Frost Middle School (Rockville, MD) 142–143
Roberts, B.W. 102
Robertson, D.E. 52–53, 56, 176
Robinson, J. 93
Ross, S. 102
Rothstein, R. 32

safety 51, **58**, 64–**65**, 108, 116, 135, 139, 150
Sawchuk, S. 76
SCAN 100–101
scenario planning 10, 164, 166–167
Schaffhauser, D. 77
school structures *see* change and conventions of schooling
schools and communities *see* community relationships
Scott, A. 107
Seale, C. 93
Sears, M.R. 102

Section 504 39–40, 54–55
sense of belonging *see* Maslow's Hierarchy of Needs
Shifrin, D. 20
shifting educational systems **168**
shuttering
Smith, A. 15
Smith, S. 152–153
social capital in a virtual world 94–95
social distancing 13, 18, 57, **58**, 62, 84, 86, 157
social emotional learning (SEL) 100, 102, 106; adult needs 108–109; CASEL competency areas **107**; child abuse 39–40, 128; coping with emotions **122**; impact of COVID-19 108–109; mental health 20, 43; role of school 63–64; safety 109, 115–116; skill development 100–101; student needs 109–**110**; webs of support 115–116, 120
social media 14–16, 24, 51, 92, 188
social networks *31*, 94, 99
Spearman, M. 26
Stancil, S. 89–90, 93, 178
Stickle, L. 106
Stirman, S.W. 65
Strauss, V. 32
student services 40–41; legal responsibilities 40; remote deliver 44; special education 41
Subramaniam, T. 15
Sullivan, K. 15, 152

Tam, G. 168
Tarasawa, B. 33
Tate, K. 107
teachers as essential workers 13–14, 132
teaching and change *see* change and conventions of schooling
teaching as human endeavor 30–31
ten Bokkel, I. 107
The Museum School of Avondale Estates (Decatur, GA) 35
Thomson, W.M. 102
traditional school structures *see* change and conventions of schooling
transportation 56–58, 72, 157, *158–159*
Troop, B. 67, 70, 176–177

Unrest *see* context of COVID
USAFacts 33

Velez, A. 109
Verdasca, J. 100
Virginia Beach City Public Schools (Virginia Beach VA) 52–53, 56
virtual learning *see* change and conventions of schooling

waivers 3, 41
Walker, T. 39
Watts, C.J. 129–130, 134, 180
Weissberg, R.P. 100, 107
Wen, H. 141
Westwood, S. 13
Wheatley, M. 4
Wiglesworth, M. 107
Woodall, C. 45
Wooden, J. 150

Zerotothree 35
Zepeda, S.J. 136

Printed in the United States
By Bookmasters